ROSE MURRAY'S
CANADIAN
Christmas Cooking
The CLASSIC GUIDE to
HOLIDAY FEASTS

ROSE MURRAY'S CANADIAN

Christmas Cooking

The CLASSIC GUIDE *to* HOLIDAY FEASTS

whitecap

Whitecap Books is known for its expertise in
the cookbook market, and has produced some
of the most innovative and familiar titles found
in kitchens across North America. Visit our
website at www.whitecap.ca.

EDITED BY Julia Aitken and Theresa Best
DESIGNED BY Michelle Furbacher
COVER DESIGN BY Andrew Bagatella and
Michelle Furbacher
COVER PHOTOGRAPHY AND FOOD
STYLING Tracey Kusiewicz
PROOFREADING Lesley Cameron
ILLUSTRATIONS istockphoto.com/elapela

Printed in Canada

LIBRARY AND ARCHIVES CANADA CATALOGUING
IN PUBLICATION
    Murray, Rose, 1941-
Rose Murray's Canadian Christmas cooking /
Rose Murray.—2nd ed.
First published (Lorimer, 1979) under title: The
Christmas cookbook.
Includes index.
ISBN 978-1-77050-192-8
1. Christmas cooking. 2. Cooking, Canadian.
3. Cookbooks. I. Title. II. Title: Canadian
Christmas cooking. III. Title: Christmas
cookbook.
TX739.2.C45M88 2013   641.5'686
C2013-900953-1

The publisher acknowledges the financial
support of the Government of Canada through
the Canada Book Fund (CBF) and the Province
of British Columbia through the Book Publishing
Tax Credit.

13 14 15 16 17 5 4 3 2 1

For Claire and Mitchell,
who make my Christmases particularly special.

Contents

Introduction

WHAT WOULD A Canadian Christmas be without custom and tradition? Even in pioneer Canada, when much of the settlers' energy was absorbed just surviving the bitter winter, considerable time was devoted to trimming trees, making gifts and preparing a traditional Christmas dinner.

In fact, custom was particularly important when it came to the food for a pioneer Christmas. By steaming a plum pudding or stuffing a goose, British settlers could forget, at least for a short time, that they were thousands of miles from their homes and families. For the same reason, Ukrainian families would spend weeks preparing the twelve meatless dishes for their Svyata Vechera (Christmas Eve supper on January 6), and Icelandic children would be introduced to the delights of Vinarterta, a multi-layered white cake with prune or date filling (see recipe page 18). Familiar Christmas dishes provided both a link to the past and a sense of ethnic identity in a vast, and often harsh, new land.

For early pioneers, finding the necessary ingredients for a traditional favourite was no easy task. Handfuls of scarce luxuries such as sugar, raisins and dried fruits were often hoarded during the fall months in readiness for that one all-important meal, Christmas dinner.

Often substitutions had to be made, and ingenious adaptations of traditional recipes resulted. When ingredients for mincemeat were scarce, for instance, apples from the cold cellar and carrots were used instead to make an unusual and delicious Winter Pie (see recipe page 43). In time, a combination of adapted recipes and traditional ethnic favourites came to form a distinctive Canadian cuisine for the Christmas season.

This new Christmas tradition in food was further enriched as recipes were exchanged between friends and neighbours of different ethnic backgrounds. The custom of baking elaborate Christmas cookies, for example, was brought to Canada by settlers of German origin and soon became popular in homes across the country.

Today Canadian Christmas cooking bears the stamp of the rich and varied Canadian tradition that has emerged since the first settlers came to this country. The recipes collected in this book pay tribute to that tradition. They were gathered from family collections from all across the country and represent both traditional ethnic favourites as well as some of the unique and delicious adaptations that originated in early Canadian homes. The menus at the end of the book are designed to help you prepare a holiday feast that reflects a wide range of ethnic favourites. Try the recipes from other cultures as well as your old standbys. This kind of exchange will enrich an already cherished holiday.

A WORD ABOUT THE RECIPES

Unless otherwise stated, all the recipes in this book were tested using unsalted butter, table salt and large eggs (except in the decorative icings, pages 20 and 58).

When using raw eggs in a recipe, choose Canada Grade A eggs within their best-before date. These eggs have come from a registered farmer and have been properly handled and graded. Use whatever milk you have on hand, except for the recipe for Scalloped Oysters (page 134), which requires whole (3.25%) milk.

A "non-reactive" bowl or saucepan (glass or stainless steel) is one that will not react chemically to its contents.

Cakes, Icings and Toppings

he custom of having cakes and other sweets at Christmas originated in England, when cakes were given to the poor women who sang carols in the streets. British settlers introduced fruitcakes to Canada, and settlers from other countries brought their traditional Christmas recipes with them, too. On Christmas Eve in Nova Scotia, for instance, village people would participate in the Dutch and German custom of "bell snicklers." Dressed in traditional costumes, they would call on their neighbours, announcing the holiday season with bells and horns and wishing all a merry Christmas and happy new year. The callers would then be invited in for singing and Christmas cakes with wine. And in Newfoundland, the mummers, troupes of professional entertainers, served cake and drinks at each village on their holiday season tour.

In Canada today, Christmas is almost the only time of year when these special cakes are made. (Wedding feasts are another time, and some of the larger fruitcakes in this chapter would be perfect for a wedding cake.)

Most people have personal favourites, often recipes that have been passed down through the generations. The cakes in this chapter have been adapted from cherished family collections from all parts of the country. They represent a variety of cultural traditions—from British to Swedish to Ukrainian—and they range in taste and size to accommodate a variety of personal preferences.

Preparing Christmas cakes is a labour of love in Canadian homes. Here are some tips that will help make that labour enjoyable and the results well worth the effort.

INGREDIENTS

For a truly successful cake, use only fresh ingredients, buying nuts and candied fruit in a store where there is brisk business, to ensure they're as fresh as possible. Try shopping at bulk stores where you can purchase only what you need for the recipe.

CANDIED (OR GLACÉ) FRUIT is preserved in a thick sugar syrup, which should look clear and bright, not cloudy, to indicate its freshness.

CANDIED PEEL is similar to candied fruit but is made from the peel and pith of citrus fruits or the peel of citron, an oblong greenish fruit with a thick, fragrant rind. Mixed peel is usually equal parts orange, lemon and citron peel.

RAISINS are dried grapes with the variety of raisin depending on the type of grape:

- Sultanas are made from seedless grapes and include the less expensive, generic sultanas, golden raisins (a Thompson grape, but treated to prevent them from darkening) and dark Thompson raisins (dark due to prolonged drying and considered the best of the seedless raisins).

- Muscat (also known as lexia) raisins are traditional big, dark, sticky raisins, loved for their rich wine flavour, that are dried from grapes with seeds. Bakers used to have to remove the seeds themselves, but there are now seedless muscat raisins available.

- Currants are not from the red, black or white berries related to the gooseberry, they are the dried grapes of a small black variety, originally from Corinth, Greece (the word "Corinth" evolved into "currant").

CAKE PANS Loaf pans have been suggested for most of the recipes that follow because they are standard equipment in most kitchens. Other pans may be used instead, but the baking time should be adjusted according to the pan size. Recipes that call for two loaf pans should fit nicely into one

13- × 9-inch (3.5 L) metal cake pan. The finished cake can be cut crosswise into six rectangular logs, which are nice for gift-giving. Since this larger pan is about half as deep as a loaf pan, cut the baking time in half but be sure to test for doneness.

BAKING FRUITCAKES I like to butter the pans for fruitcakes, then line them with two layers of buttered parchment paper. The double layer of paper prevents the bottoms and sides of the cakes from drying out during the long baking time. A shallow roasting pan of hot water placed in the oven while a fruitcake bakes will help to keep it moist. If the top of the cake appears to be drying out, simply place a double layer of parchment paper over the top.

TESTING A FRUITCAKE FOR DONENESS Baking time varies according to the pan size, the richness of the batter and how accurate your oven's temperature is. To avoid over-baking a fruitcake, test it by inserting a skewer into the middle of the cake at least half an hour before the end of the recommended baking time. The skewer should not come out gummy with batter, although remember it may be sticky because of the fruit.

STORING A FRUITCAKE Most cakes become moist and mellow and improve in flavour if they are baked a few weeks before they are to be served. Storing is an important factor in the success of a fruitcake.

For best results, ripen the cake: Let the cake cool completely after it has come out of the oven. Make several holes down through the cake with a skewer and pour in heated (but not boiled) brandy. Moisten a piece of cheesecloth large enough to enclose the cake with sherry or brandy (not table wine) and wrap it around the cake. Finally, wrap the cake in foil and store it in an airtight container in the refrigerator for up to a year.

Although there is no need to freeze a fruitcake, the refrigerated cake should be checked periodically to ensure that it hasn't become too moist or too dry. If it is too moist, there is a danger of its becoming mouldy. To avoid this, let the cake air for a while. If the cake becomes dry, moisten the cheesecloth again with sherry or brandy.

White Coconut Fruitcake

Makes two 9- × 5-inch (23 × 12 cm) cakes

This small white fruitcake has been one of my favourites for years.
It is very moist and filled with fruit and nuts.

....

3 cups (750 mL) golden sultana raisins

3 cups (750 mL) diced mixed candied fruit

1½ cups (375 mL) halved red and green candied cherries

1½ cups (375 mL) diced candied pineapple

1 cup (250 mL) unsweetened desiccated coconut

1 cup (250 mL) blanched slivered almonds

2 cups (500 mL) all purpose flour, divided

2 tsp (10 mL) baking powder

½ tsp (2 mL) salt

½ cup (125 mL) butter, softened

1 cup (250 mL) granulated sugar

3 eggs

1 tsp (5 mL) almond extract

⅓ cup (75 mL) orange juice

¼ cup (60 mL) brandy

PREPARE TWO 9- × 5-inch (2 L) loaf pans by greasing them with butter and lining them with two layers of buttered parchment paper. Preheat the oven to 250°F (120°C).

Combine all the fruit and nuts in a large bowl and toss them with ¼ cup (60 mL) of the flour.

In a medium bowl, sift the remaining flour with the baking powder and salt.

In a large bowl, cream the butter, add the granulated sugar and beat until light and fluffy. Add the eggs, one at a time, beating well after each addition. Stir in the almond extract.

Stir in the orange juice and brandy alternately with the sifted dry ingredients. Fold in the floured fruit and nuts.

Scrape the batter into the prepared pans and bake for 3 hours or until a skewer inserted in the middle of each cake comes out clean.

Cool the cakes for 30 minutes in the pans, then turn out onto racks. Carefully remove the paper and cool completely.

Brazil Nut Fruitcake

Makes four 9- × 5-inch (23 × 12 cm) cakes

Crammed full of fruit and whole Brazil nuts, this large moist fruitcake
not only makes a beautiful Christmas cake but is also perfect as a
wedding cake. Make sure the Brazil nuts are very fresh as rancid ones
will spoil the taste of your cake.

....

3 cups (750 mL) red candied
  cherries
3 cups (750 mL) green
  candied cherries
6 cups (1.5 L) golden sultana
  raisins
4 cups (1 L) whole Brazil nuts

3 cups (750 mL) diced mixed
  candied fruit
4½ cups (1.12 L) all-purpose
  flour, divided
2 cups (500 mL) butter,
  softened
2 cups (500 mL) granulated
  sugar

12 eggs, separated
1 Tbsp (15 mL) almond
  extract
2 tsp (10 mL) baking powder
½ tsp (2 mL) salt
2 cups (500 mL) crushed
  canned pineapple,
  undrained

CUT THE CHERRIES into halves or quarters,
then, in a large bowl, toss the cherries,
raisins, nuts and candied fruit with ½ cup
(125 mL) of the flour. Let this mixture sit
overnight so that the flavours can mingle.

When you are ready to bake the cakes,
prepare four 9- × 5-inch (2 L) loaf pans (or
other pans of your choice) by greasing them
with butter and lining them with two layers
of buttered parchment paper. Preheat the
oven to 250°F (120°C).

In a large bowl, cream the butter
thoroughly and add the sugar gradually,
beating until light and fluffy.

In a separate bowl, beat the egg whites
until stiff but still moist. Set aside. In
another bowl, beat the egg yolks and add
them to the creamed mixture. Stir in the
almond extract.

In a medium bowl, sift the remaining
flour with the baking powder and salt. Add
the dry ingredients to the creamed mixture
a bit at a time, stirring only to blend after
each addition. Mix in the crushed pineapple
and its juice, and stir in the prepared fruit
and nuts. Fold in the beaten egg whites.

Scrape the batter into the prepared
pans and bake for about 3½ hours or until a
skewer inserted in the middle of each cake
comes out clean.

Cool the cakes for 30 minutes in the
pans then turn out onto racks. Carefully
remove the paper and cool completely.

Use the almond paste and icing recipes
at the end of this chapter to decorate the
cakes before serving.

Rich Ginger-Pecan Fruitcake

Makes four 9- × 5-inch (23 × 12 cm) cakes

The distinctive taste of ginger and the rich flavour of pecans give this
medium-light fruitcake a special appeal. Since there is no baking powder
or baking soda in this cake, its texture will be somewhat dense.

....

3 cups (750 mL) granulated
   sugar, divided
1 cup (250 mL) water
1 Tbsp (15 mL) corn syrup
4 cups (1 L) pecan halves
3 cups (750 mL) golden
   sultana raisins
3 cups (750 mL) chopped red
   candied cherries
3 cups (750 mL) chopped
   green candied cherries

2⅔ cups (650 mL) chopped
   candied pineapple
2⅓ cups (575 mL) diced
   candied citron peel
2¼ cups (550 mL) blanched
   almond halves
1 cup (250 mL) diced candied
   orange peel
¾ cup (175 mL) chopped
   candied ginger (one 6 oz/
   175 mL jar, drained)

½ cup (125 mL) diced candied
   lemon peel
1 cup (250 mL) brandy
2 cups (500 mL) butter,
   softened
4 cups (1 L) all-purpose flour
8 eggs

MAKE A SYRUP by boiling ½ cup (125 mL) of the sugar with the water in a small saucepan for 5 minutes. Add the corn syrup and set aside.

Place the pecans, raisins, cherries, pineapple, citron peel, almonds, orange peel, ginger and lemon peel in a large glass bowl. Add ½ cup (125 mL) of the syrup and all of the brandy. Stir to mix thoroughly, cover tightly and let sit for 24 hours, stirring occasionally.

When you are ready to bake the cakes, prepare four 9- × 5-inch (2 L) loaf pans (or other pans of your choice) by greasing them with butter and lining them with two layers of buttered parchment paper. Preheat the oven to 250°F (120°C).

In a large bowl, cream the butter well. Gradually add the flour, creaming to blend smoothly.

In a medium bowl, beat the eggs lightly and gradually beat in the remaining sugar. Add the egg mixture to the creamed mixture, stirring just until blended. Gradually add the nut and fruit mixture, gently folding and mixing the ingredients together with your hands.

Scrape the batter into the prepared pans and bake for about 4 hours or until a skewer inserted in the middle of each cake comes out clean.

Cool the cakes for 30 minutes in the pans, then turn out onto racks. Carefully remove the paper and cool completely.

Although this cake is moist and delicious after a few days, let it ripen for 3 to 4 weeks for best results (see page 4). Use the almond paste and icing recipes at the end of this chapter to decorate the cake before serving.

Cherry Cake

Makes one 9- × 5-inch (23 × 12 cm) cake

The almonds and coconut in this cake give it an unusual crunchy texture.
This is a small, light cake, not heavily loaded with fruit.

··

½ cup (125 mL) butter,
softened
1 cup (250 mL) granulated
sugar
3 eggs, separated
1 tsp (5 mL) cherry extract
1¼ cups (300 mL) chopped
blanched almonds

¾ cup (175 mL) whole
candied cherries
⅓ cup (75 mL) diced candied
citron peel
¼ cup (60 mL) unsweetened
shredded coconut
1¾ cups (425 mL) all-purpose
flour, divided

1 tsp (5 mL) baking powder
¼ tsp (1 mL) salt
¼ cup (60 mL) milk

PREPARE A 9- × 5-inch (2 L) loaf pan by greasing it with butter and lining it with two layers of buttered parchment paper. Preheat the oven to 275°F (140°C).

In a large bowl, cream the butter, gradually add the sugar and beat until light and fluffy.

In a medium bowl, beat the egg yolks well and add to the creamed mixture. Stir in the cherry extract.

In another medium bowl, toss the almonds, cherries, citron peel and coconut with ¼ cup (60 mL) of the flour.

In a small bowl, sift the remaining flour with the baking powder and salt. Slowly add the dry ingredients, alternating with the milk, to the creamed mixture. Stir in the prepared nuts and fruit.

In a clean medium bowl with clean beaters, beat the egg whites until stiff but still moist, and carefully fold them into the batter (the batter should be quite stiff). Scrape the batter into the prepared pan.

Bake for about 3 hours or until a skewer inserted in the middle of the cake comes out clean.

Cool the cake for 20 minutes in the pan, then turn out onto a rack. Carefully remove the paper and cool completely.

Use the almond paste and icing recipes at the end of this chapter to decorate the cake before serving.

Spicy Apricot-Pecan Fruitcake

Makes two 9- × 5-inch (23 × 12 cm) cakes and one 5- × 3-inch (12 × 8 cm) cake

This spicy fruitcake has a more cake-like texture than some of the others in this chapter. The batter for this cake will fill two 9- × 5-inch (2 L) loaf pans, plus a smaller pan, such as a mini loaf pan or coffee can, which makes a small cake suitable for gift-giving.

....

4 cups (1 L) muscat raisins
2 cups (500 mL) currants
1½ cups (375 mL) golden sultana raisins
1½ cups (375 mL) diced mixed peel
1½ cups (375 mL) granulated sugar
1½ cups (375 mL) apricot nectar

1 cup (250 mL) chopped dried apricots
1 cup (250 mL) chopped pecans
¾ cup (175 mL) diced candied cherries
⅔ cup (150 mL) chopped candied pineapple
1 cup (250 mL) butter
3 eggs

2½ cups (625 mL) all-purpose flour
1 tsp (5 mL) baking powder
1 tsp (5 mL) baking soda
1 tsp (5 mL) cinnamon
1 tsp (5 mL) ground allspice
1 tsp (5 mL) ground mace
½ tsp (2 mL) salt

IN A LARGE heavy-bottomed saucepan, combine the raisins, currants, sultana raisins, mixed peel, sugar, apricot nectar, apricots, pecans, cherries and pineapple. Bring to a boil, then boil, stirring constantly, for 5 minutes. Remove from the heat, add the butter and stir well. Cool. The flavours will blend better if this mixture is allowed to sit overnight.

Prepare two 9- × 5-inch (2 L) loaf pans and a 5- × 3-inch (500 mL) mini loaf pan (or a 1 lb/500 g coffee can) by greasing them with butter and lining them with two layers of buttered parchment paper. Preheat the oven to 300°F (150°C).

In a medium bowl, beat the eggs thoroughly and add them to the fruit mixture.

In another medium bowl, sift together the flour, baking powder, baking soda, spices and salt. Add the dry ingredients to the fruit mixture and stir well to combine. Scrape the batter into the prepared pans, leaving room for the batter to rise.

Bake for 2 to 2½ hours for the larger loaf pans, for 30 to 45 minutes for the mini loaf pan or coffee can, or until a skewer inserted in the middle of each cake comes out clean.

Cool the cakes for 30 minutes in the pans, then turn out onto racks. Carefully remove the paper and cool completely.

Use the almond paste and icing recipes at the end of this chapter to decorate the cakes before serving.

Dark Rum-Nut Fruitcake

Makes four 9- × 5-inch (23 × 12 cm) cakes

Soaking the fruit and nuts overnight allows the flavours of this moist,
yet dense cake to mingle.

....

6 cups (1.5 L) diced mixed
    candied peel
6 cups (1.5 L) Thompson
    raisins
4 cups (1 L) currants
2 cups (500 mL) blanched
    slivered almonds
2 cups (500 mL) coarsely
    chopped walnuts

1½ cups (375 mL) diced
    candied citron peel
1½ cups (375 mL) halved red
    candied cherries
1½ cups (375 mL) halved
    green candied cherries
1 cup (250 mL) dark rum
3½ cups (875 mL) all-
    purpose flour, divided

2 cups (500 mL) butter,
    softened
2½ cups (625 mL) lightly
    packed brown sugar
7 eggs
1 Tbsp (15 mL) vanilla
2 tsp (10 mL) baking powder
½ tsp (2 mL) salt
2 tsp (10 mL) cinnamon
1 tsp (5 mL) ground cloves

IN A LARGE glass bowl, combine all the
peel, fruit and nuts. Pour the rum over the
mixture and mix thoroughly. Cover and let
sit overnight.

When you are ready to bake the cakes,
prepare four 9- × 5-inch (2 L) loaf pans (or
other pans of your choice) by greasing them
with butter and lining them with two layers
of buttered parchment paper. Preheat the
oven to 250°F (120°C).

Drain any liquid from the fruit and set
it aside. Toss the fruit with ½ cup (125 mL)
of the flour.

In another large bowl, cream the butter,
add the brown sugar and beat until light
and fluffy. Add the eggs, one at a time,
beating thoroughly after each addition. Stir

in the vanilla and reserved liquid from the
fruit.

In a medium bowl, sift the remaining
flour with the baking powder, salt,
cinnamon and cloves. Gradually add to the
creamed mixture, stirring just to blend. Stir
in the floured fruit and nuts.

Scrape the batter into the prepared pans
and bake for 3 to 3½ hours or until a skewer
inserted in the middle of each cake comes
out clean.

Cool the cakes for 30 minutes in the
pans, then turn out onto racks. Carefully
remove the paper and cool completely.

Use the almond paste and icing recipes
at the end of this chapter to decorate the
cakes before serving.

Banana Fruitcake

Makes two 9- × 5-inch (23 × 12 cm) cakes

A very moist cake with a rich spicy flavour, this fruitcake
will ripen completely within two weeks. In fact, the flavour
and texture are good the day it is baked.

....

3 cups (750 mL) chopped
mixed candied fruit
2 cups (500 mL) chopped
pitted dates
1 cup (250 mL) chopped
walnuts
½ cup (125 mL) chopped
candied pineapple
2½ cups (625 mL) all-
purpose flour, divided

1 tsp (5 mL) baking powder
1 tsp (5 mL) baking soda
1 tsp (5 mL) salt
1 tsp (5 mL) cinnamon
¼ tsp (1 mL) freshly grated
nutmeg
¼ tsp (1 mL) ground cloves
¾ cup (175 mL) butter,
softened

2 cups (500 mL) lightly
packed brown sugar
4 eggs
1 Tbsp (15 mL) orange juice
1 tsp (5 mL) grated orange
zest
½ tsp (2 mL) orange extract
1½ cups (375 mL) mashed
ripe bananas*

PREPARE TWO 9- × 5-inch (2 L) loaf pans
by greasing them with butter and lining
them with two layers of buttered parchment
paper. Preheat the oven to 300°F (150°C).

In a large bowl, combine the candied
fruit, dates, walnuts and pineapple. Toss
them with ¼ cup (60 mL) of the flour.

In a medium bowl, sift the remaining
flour with the baking powder, baking soda,
salt, cinnamon, nutmeg and cloves. Set
aside.

In a large bowl, cream the butter, add
the sugar and beat until the mixture is light
and fluffy. Beat in the eggs, one at a time.
Beat in the orange juice, orange zest and
orange extract.

Stir the bananas into the creamed
mixture alternately with the flour mixture.
Stir in the floured fruit and nuts.

Scrape the batter into the prepared pans
and bake for 2¼ hours or until a skewer
inserted in the middle of each cake comes
out clean.

Cool the cakes for 20 minutes in the
pans, then turn out onto racks. Carefully
remove the paper and cool completely.

* Use a fork, not a food processor, to mash
the bananas. A food processor will liquefy
the bananas, which will change the texture
of the cake.

Black Bun

Makes one 8-inch (20 cm) cake

This Scottish fruitcake enclosed in pastry is probably less
familiar to Canadians than Dundee cake. Although it is traditionally
served on New Year's Eve, this is an interesting and attractive cake
to have on hand all through the holiday season.

....

PASTRY
2½ cups (625 mL) all-
  purpose flour
¾ tsp (4 mL) baking powder
1 cup (250 mL) chilled butter,
  cut into tiny pieces
6 to 8 Tbsp (90 to 120 mL)
  ice water

CAKE
4 cups (1 L) all-purpose flour
1 tsp (5 mL) cinnamon
1 tsp (5 mL) ground ginger

1 tsp (5 mL) baking soda
½ tsp (2 mL) freshly ground
  black pepper
¼ tsp (1 mL) ground cloves
¼ tsp (1 mL) salt
6 cups (1.5 L) Thompson
  raisins
3½ cups (875 mL) currants
2 cups (500 mL) muscat
  raisins
1 cup (250 mL) diced mixed
  candied peel

1 cup (250 mL) blanched
  slivered almonds
2 eggs
1 cup (250 mL) lightly packed
  brown sugar
1 cup (250 mL) buttermilk*
½ cup (125 mL) brandy
1 egg, slightly beaten

TO MAKE THE PASTRY, combine the flour
and baking powder in a medium bowl. Rub
the butter into the flour until the mixture
resembles coarse rolled oats. Be sure that
your hands are not too warm when doing
this and work as quickly as possible. Pour in
6 Tbsp (90 mL) of the ice water. Shape the
dough into a ball but do not overwork it. If
it crumbles too much, add 1 to 2 Tbsp (15
to 30 mL) more of ice water. Wrap and chill
the dough for 1 to 2 hours.

Prepare an 8-inch (20 cm) round cake
pan that's 3 inches (8 cm) deep by buttering
the bottom and sides. Preheat the oven to
350°F (180°C).

Break off two-thirds of the chilled
pastry. On a lightly floured board roll it
out into a disc approximately 16 inches
(40 cm) in diameter and ¼ inch (6 mm)
thick. Gently press the pastry into the
prepared pan, being careful not to stretch

it. Trim off the excess dough, leaving a
tiny rim all around the pan. Roll out the
remaining pastry into a 10-inch (25 cm)
disc and set aside for the top.

To make the cake, sift the flour,
cinnamon, ginger, baking soda, pepper,
cloves and salt into a large bowl. Add the
Thompson raisins, currants, muscat raisins,
peel and almonds. Mix well to coat with the
flour.

In a medium bowl, beat the eggs, add
the brown sugar and beat well together. Stir
in the buttermilk and brandy. Add the egg
mixture to the flour and fruit mixture and
combine everything well.

Spoon the batter into the pastry-lined
pan. Cover with the pastry top but be
careful not to stretch it. Seal tightly to the
tiny rim of pastry around the pan and crimp
slightly with your fingers or the tines of a
fork. With a fork, prick the pastry all over

the top and cut two small slits in the centre with a sharp knife. Brush the top with beaten egg.

Bake for 1½ hours. Reduce the temperature to 275°F (140°C) and bake for another 1½ hours or until the top is golden brown. Cool completely in the pan, then carefully remove and cover tightly with foil.

Let the cake sit at room temperature for a week before serving. The cake can be stored for 3 to 4 weeks and freezes well.

* If buttermilk is unavailable, stir 2 tsp (10 mL) fresh lemon juice or white vinegar into 1 cup (250 mL) milk and let stand for 10 minutes before using.

Dundee Cake

Makes one 9- × 5-inch (23 × 12 cm) cake

This white Scottish fruitcake was well known to many early Canadian settlers. It's a delicate cake with just a smattering of fruit.

....

2½ cups (625 mL) all-purpose flour
1 tsp (5 mL) baking powder
½ tsp (2 mL) salt
⅔ cup (150 mL) chopped maraschino cherries

1 cup (250 mL) golden sultana raisins
1⅓ cups (325 mL) currants
1 cup (250 mL) butter, softened
⅔ cup (150 mL) granulated sugar

4 eggs
1 Tbsp (15 mL) fresh lemon juice
½ tsp (2 mL) almond extract

PREPARE A 9- × 5-inch (2 L) loaf pan by greasing it with butter and lining it with two layers of buttered parchment paper. Preheat the oven to 275°F (140°C).

In a medium bowl, sift together the flour, baking powder and salt.

Drain the cherries thoroughly in a sieve then pat dry on paper towels. In a second medium bowl, combine the cherries with the raisins and currants and toss the fruit with ¼ cup (60 mL) of the dry ingredients.

In a large bowl, cream the butter, add the sugar and beat until light and fluffy. Add the eggs, one at a time, beating well after each addition. Stir in the lemon juice and almond extract.

Gradually stir the dry ingredients into the creamed mixture, mixing only to blend. Stir in the prepared fruit.

Scrape the batter into the prepared pan and bake for 2 hours or until a skewer inserted in the middle of the cake comes out clean.

Cool the cake for 20 minutes in the pan, then turn out onto a rack. Carefully remove the paper and cool completely.

Use the almond paste and icing recipes at the end of this chapter to decorate the cake before serving.

Old-Fashioned Pound Cake

Makes one 9- × 5-inch (23 × 12 cm) cake

Pound cake got its name because all of the ingredients—butter, sugar, eggs and flour—each weighed one pound. In some early households, particularly in the Maritimes, there always had to be a pound cake at Christmas.

It was said that the cake was best if made by two people—one to beat the sugar and butter, the other to sift the flour and beat the eggs. This co-operative effort by neighbours was quite practical because the more the pound cake was beaten, the finer the texture and the lighter the cake, since no baking powder or baking soda was used to help it rise. Like those original recipes, this pound cake is made without any leavening. An electric mixer will incorporate air into the batter if no helpful neighbour is available.

....

1 cup (250 mL) butter, softened
1 cup (250 mL) granulated sugar
5 eggs, separated

2 tsp (10 mL) grated lemon zest
1½ Tbsp (22 mL) fresh lemon juice
1 Tbsp (15 mL) brandy

1 tsp (5 mL) vanilla
2¼ cups (550 mL) all-purpose flour

PREPARE A 9- × 5-inch (2 L) loaf pan by greasing it with butter and lining it with one layer of buttered parchment paper. Preheat the oven to 325°F (160°C).

In a large bowl, and using an electric mixer, cream the butter until very smooth. Gradually add the sugar, beating well until very light and fluffy.

In a medium bowl, and using an electric mixer, beat the egg yolks until light-coloured and creamy. Beat in the lemon zest, lemon juice, brandy and vanilla. Beat this mixture well into the butter and sugar mixture. Very gradually stir in the flour.

Using clean beaters, beat the egg whites in a large bowl until they are stiff but not dry. Fold them into the batter, one-third at a time.

Spoon the batter into the prepared pan and bake for 1 hour and 20 minutes or until light golden brown and a skewer inserted in the middle of the cake comes out clean.

Cool the cake for 10 minutes in the pan, then turn out onto a rack. Carefully remove the parchment paper and cool completely.

The cake keeps well wrapped in brandy-soaked cheesecloth in an airtight container. It does not freeze well.

Christmas Medivnyk

(UKRAINIAN HONEY CAKE)

Makes 12 servings

Cakes and pastries made with honey are a tradition at the
Ukrainian Christmas Eve supper, called Svyata Vechera,
which takes place on January 6. For the most authentically rich
colour and flavour, use buckwheat honey for this cake, which stays
deliciously moist for days.

....

1 cup (250 mL) honey
½ cup (125 mL) butter,
  softened
1 cup (250 mL) lightly packed
  brown sugar
4 eggs, separated
3 cups (750 mL) all-purpose
  flour

1 tsp (5 mL) cinnamon
1 tsp (5 mL) baking powder
½ tsp (2 mL) ground cloves
¼ tsp (1 mL) freshly grated
  nutmeg
¼ tsp (1 mL) salt
1 cup (250 mL) sour cream

2 tsp (10 mL) baking soda
1 cup (250 mL) chopped
  walnuts
Icing sugar
Sweetened whipped cream

PREPARE A 10-inch (4 L) tube pan by
greasing it with butter. Preheat the oven to
325°F (160°C).

Bring the honey to a boil in a small
saucepan, then let it cool.

In a large bowl, cream the butter. Add
the brown sugar and beat until light and
fluffy. Add the egg yolks, one at a time,
beating well after each addition. Beat in the
cooled honey.

In a medium bowl, sift together the
flour, cinnamon, baking powder, cloves,
nutmeg and salt.

In a separate medium bowl, beat the
egg whites until stiff but still moist. In a
small bowl, stir together the sour cream and
baking soda.

Add the dry ingredients to the creamed
mixture alternately with the sour cream.
Stir in the walnuts. Fold in the stiffly beaten
egg whites.

Spoon the batter into the prepared
pan. Bake for 40 minutes. Reduce the
temperature to 300°F (150°C) and bake for
30 to 35 minutes longer or until a skewer
inserted in the middle of the cake comes
out clean.

Cool the cake for 20 minutes in the
pan, then turn out onto a rack and cool
completely. Wrap the cake in plastic wrap,
then let it ripen in an airtight container for
a day before serving. Just before serving,
sprinkle the cake with icing sugar and top it
with whipped cream.

Bûche de Noël

(YULE LOG)

Makes 10 to 12 servings

A traditional French holiday cake, this is made and decorated to resemble
the yule log, which burns in the hearth to denote friendliness and
warmth. Bûche de Noël is often served in French-Canadian homes as a
spectacular ending for the Christmas Eve dinner.

CAKE
1¼ cups (300 mL) granulated
  sugar, divided
1 cup (250 mL) cake-and-
  pastry flour
4 eggs, separated
¼ tsp (1 mL) salt
1 tsp (5 mL) vanilla
Icing sugar

RUM SYRUP
¼ cup (60 mL) granulated
  sugar
¼ cup (60 mL) water

1 Tbsp (15 mL) dark rum

COFFEE CREAM
3 egg yolks
⅔ cup (150 mL) granulated
  sugar
½ cup (125 mL) water
1 cup (250 mL) butter,
  softened
1½ Tbsp (22 mL) dark rum
1 Tbsp (15 mL) very strong
  black coffee

CHOCOLATE BUTTER ICING
¼ cup (60 mL) butter, softened

2 cups (500 mL) sifted icing
  sugar
½ tsp (2 mL) vanilla
Pinch of salt
2 Tbsp (30 mL) half-and-
  half (10%) or table (18%)
  cream
2 squares unsweetened
  chocolate, melted (2 oz/
  60 g)
Candied cherries and candied
  citron peel or angelica

TO MAKE THE CAKE, prepare a 15- × 10-inch
(38 × 25 cm) jelly-roll pan by greasing it with
butter, lining it with one layer of buttered
parchment paper and sprinkling it with flour.
Preheat the oven to 400°F (200°C).

In a medium bowl, whisk together 1 cup
(250 mL) of the sugar and the flour.

In a separate medium bowl, beat the egg
whites with the salt until stiff. Gradually
beat in the remaining sugar.

In a large bowl, beat the egg yolks until
thick. Beat in the vanilla. Fold in the stiffly
beaten egg whites, then gradually fold in
the flour mixture, a bit at a time.

Spoon the batter into the prepared pan
and spread it evenly. Bake for 15 minutes
or until the cake springs back when lightly
pressed.

Sprinkle a clean tea towel with icing
sugar. Turn the hot cake out onto the towel
and carefully remove the pan and paper.
Trim any hard edges from the cake. Roll
the cake and towel up from a long side and
cool. The roll should be long and thin.

Meanwhile, make the rum syrup by
boiling the sugar and water together in a
small saucepan for about 3 minutes or until
syrupy. The syrup will burn if cooked too
long, so watch it carefully. Cool and add the
rum.

To make the coffee cream, beat the egg
yolks in a medium heatproof bowl until
thick. In a small heavy-bottomed saucepan,
boil together the sugar and water until the
mixture registers 240°F (115°C) on a candy
thermometer and forms a soft ball when a

Gradually beat the hot syrup into the egg yolks and continue beating until the mixture is lukewarm. Add the butter, bit by bit, still beating constantly. Beat in the rum and coffee. Let cool completely and chill briefly if too runny.

Unroll the cake and brush it with half of the rum syrup. Reserving ¼ cup (60 mL), spread the coffee cream evenly over the cake. Roll up the cake like a jelly roll. Wrap it in wax paper and chill until the coffee cream is firm.

To make the chocolate butter icing, cream the butter in a large bowl. Add about half the icing sugar and beat until fluffy. Add the vanilla and salt. Stir in the remaining sugar alternately with the cream. Blend in the chocolate. Beat until the icing stands in sharp peaks. If the icing is too stiff, add a bit more cream.

Unwrap the rolled cake. Cut a small diagonal slice from each end of the cake. These slices will make the knots in the log.

Brush the outside of the cake and the knots with the rest of the rum syrup. Attach the knots to the top of the log (the rum syrup will act as glue). Using the reserved coffee cream, decorate the ends of the knots and the ends of the log.

Spread the rest of the cake with some of the chocolate butter icing. Using a pastry bag filled with the remaining icing, decorate the log and knots to look like bark. (Alternatively, spread the icing smoothly over the entire log and run a fork along the length of the log to resemble bark.) Decorate the finished log with candied cherries and candied citron peel or angelica cut to resemble holly leaves.

Store the finished cake in a cool place until serving time so that the coffee cream does not become too soft. If you store it in the refrigerator, let the cake return to room temperature before serving.

Vinarterta

Makes 24 servings

Vinarterta is an Icelandic Christmas torte that gets better the longer
you keep it. Although the cake is dry when first baked, it becomes more
moist and flavourful if left, well covered, for at least a week.
This particular version is from an Icelandic community in Saskatchewan.
You'll need six 9-inch (1.5 L) round pans for this cake. If you don't
have six, bake the cake in batches.

....

CAKE
½ cup (125 mL) lard, softened
½ cup (125 mL) butter,
  softened
1½ cups (375 mL) granulated
  sugar
3 eggs
3 Tbsp (45 mL) table (18%)
  cream
1 Tbsp (15 mL) almond extract
3½ cups (875 mL) cake-and-
  pastry flour

1 Tbsp (15 mL) baking powder
1 tsp (5 mL) ground
  cardamom

FILLING
1 lb (500 g) chopped pitted
  dates
¾ cup (175 mL) granulated
  sugar
½ cup (125 mL) water

1 Tbsp (15 mL) fresh lemon
  juice
1 tsp (5 mL) vanilla

ICING
1 cup (250 mL) icing sugar
2 Tbsp (30 mL) butter,
  softened
3 Tbsp (45 mL) hot water
½ tsp (2 mL) almond extract

PREPARE SIX 9-inch (1.5 L) round cake pans
by greasing them with butter and sprinkling
them with flour. (Or bake the cake batter
in a couple of batches.) Preheat the oven to
375°F (190°C).

To make the cake, cream the lard and
butter in a large bowl. Add the sugar and
beat until light and fluffy. Add the eggs,
one at a time, beating well after each
addition. Stir in the cream and almond
extract.

In a medium bowl, sift together the
flour, baking powder and cardamom, and
stir into the creamed mixture. The batter
will be very stiff.

Divide the batter evenly among the
prepared pans, patting it into each one
using a circular motion. Since the batter is
so stiff, it will be difficult to spread. Bake
for 12 to 15 minutes or until golden brown.

Remove the cakes from the pans and cool
on racks.

To make the filling, combine the dates,
sugar and water in a medium saucepan.
Cook over low heat for about 5 minutes
until smooth and thick. Remove from the
heat. Stir in the lemon juice and vanilla and
cool.

Spread the top of five cakes evenly with
the date mixture. Stack the cakes one on
top of each other, finishing with the sixth
cake.

To make the icing, cream together the
icing sugar and butter in a medium bowl.
Stir in the hot water and almond extract to
make a smooth, thin icing. Pour and spread
the icing over the top of the cake, letting it
drip down the sides. Serve the torte cut into
very thin slices.

The traditional filling for Vinarterta is made with prunes but I prefer using dates. If you'd rather include prunes, substitute 1 lb (500 g) pitted prunes for the dates in the recipe, or use half prunes and half dates.

Sour Cream Coffee Cake

Makes 10 to 12 servings

This moist coffee cake is great for company and freezes well. To serve, thaw the cake overnight, then wrap it tightly in foil and heat in a 350°F (180°C) oven for 20 minutes.

....

TOPPING
⅓ cup (75 mL) butter, softened
1 cup (250 mL) icing sugar
½ cup (125 mL) all-purpose flour
½ cup (125 mL) finely chopped pecans or walnuts
2½ tsp (12 mL) cinnamon
1 tsp (5 mL) grated orange zest
1 tsp (5 mL) grated lemon zest

CAKE
½ cup (125 mL) butter, softened
1 cup (250 mL) granulated sugar
2 eggs
1 tsp (5 mL) vanilla
2 cups (500 mL) all-purpose flour
1 tsp (5 mL) baking powder
¼ tsp (1 mL) salt
1 cup (250 mL) sour cream
1 tsp (5 mL) baking soda

PREPARE A 13- × 9-inch (3.5 L) baking pan by greasing it with butter. Preheat the oven to 350°F (180°C).

To make the topping, cream the butter in a medium bowl and add the icing sugar. Stir in the flour, nuts, cinnamon and orange and lemon zests. The mixture doesn't need to be smooth. Set aside.

To make the cake, cream the butter in a large bowl. Add the granulated sugar and beat until light and fluffy. Beat in the eggs, one at a time, then beat in the vanilla.

In a medium bowl, sift together the flour, baking powder and salt.

In a small bowl, stir together the sour cream and baking soda.

Stir half of the dry ingredients into the creamed mixture. Add the sour cream mixture, then stir in the remaining dry ingredients.

Spoon the batter into the prepared pan, spreading evenly. Sprinkle the topping evenly over the top and bake for 35 minutes or until a skewer inserted in the middle of the cake comes out clean. Serve warm.

Traditional Almond Paste

Makes about 3 cups (750 mL) almond paste; enough to cover a 9-inch (23 cm) square fruitcake

Packed with all manner of moist and flavourful fruit and nuts, fruitcakes are delicious on their own but if you want to dress them up for gifts or special occasions, a layer of almond paste or almond paste plus an icing will make these cakes even more festive.

....

3 cups (750 mL) ground almonds

3 egg yolks, slightly beaten
1 Tbsp (15 mL) corn syrup

3 cups (750 mL) icing sugar
2 tsp (10 mL) almond extract

IN A LARGE BOWL, combine the ingredients in the order listed. Blend well, using your hands when necessary. Sprinkle your work surface lightly with icing sugar and turn the paste out onto it, kneading until smooth and sprinkling on more icing sugar if the mixture becomes too sticky.

To cover a fruitcake with almond paste, roll out the paste to ¼-inch (6 mm) thickness. Invert the cake onto the paste and trim the paste to fit the top of the cake. If you wish to put paste on the sides as well, cut a strip of paste to fit. If the paste does not adhere well to the fruitcake, brush the cake thinly with egg white. Allow the cake to stand overnight before adding any icing.

Royal Frosting

Makes 1⅓ cups (325 mL) frosting; enough to cover a 9- × 5-inch (23 × 12 cm) fruitcake

Spread this decorative frosting over the fruitcake after you have applied the almond paste. For best results, let the almond paste set overnight on the cake before adding the frosting.

....

2 pasteurized egg whites
¼ tsp (1 mL) cream of tartar

2¼ cups (550 mL) sifted icing sugar

½ tsp (2 mL) vanilla

IN A MEDIUM BOWL, beat the egg whites until frothy. Add the cream of tartar and continue beating until very stiff.

Sift the icing sugar through a fine sieve.

Add it, a little at a time, to the egg whites, beating for about 5 minutes, first with an electric mixer then with a wooden spoon. Beat in the vanilla.

Fluffy Fruitcake Icing

Makes about 3½ cups (875 mL) icing; enough to frost a three-layer wedding cake

After covering the top of the fruitcake with almond paste,
let the cake sit overnight before applying this fluffy frosting.

···

1 cup (250 mL) shortening,
  softened
1 tsp (5 mL) almond extract
  (or other flavouring)

1 tsp (5 mL) vanilla
8 cups (2 L) icing sugar

½ cup (125 mL) half-and-half
  (10%) cream

IN A LARGE BOWL, cream the shortening well by beating it with an electric mixer. Beat in the almond extract and vanilla. Continue beating, gradually adding the icing sugar and beating until smooth. Gradually beat in the cream until the frosting is smooth and spreads easily. You may need a little more or less cream, depending on the consistency of the frosting.

Apply a thin layer of frosting to the almond-paste-covered fruitcake. Let the frosting dry, then apply a second thick layer, smoothing the icing with a knife dipped in hot water.

Fruitcake Glaze

Makes about 1⅓ cups (325 mL) glaze; enough to decorate the tops
of four medium-sized fruitcakes

This clear glaze is less perishable than icing and can be decorated
with an arrangement of candied fruit. Cherries, pineapple and nuts make
attractive and appealing decorations for light and dark fruitcakes.

···

1 cup (250 mL) granulated
  sugar

½ cup (125 mL) water

⅓ cup (75 mL) corn syrup

IN A MEDIUM heavy-bottomed saucepan, stir together the sugar, water and corn syrup over low heat until the sugar has dissolved. Increase the heat to medium-high and boil the mixture until it registers 236°F (115°C) on a candy thermometer and forms a soft ball when a little of the mixture is dropped into a bowl of cold water.

Brush the glaze over the top of the fruitcake, reserving some of the liquid for the final glaze. Immediately arrange candied fruit and nuts on top of the cake and brush with the rest of the glaze.

Puddings, Desserts and Sweet Sauces

hether it was a lumber camp pudding made from cornmeal and the year's small supply of raisins, or an aristocratic maple sugar cake with nuts and sunflower seeds, desserts were an important part of early Canadian Christmas dinners.

New settlers brought with them a variety of recipes for cakes, custards and puddings. Most important among them was the plum pudding brought by the British; it provided a much-needed link with Christmases in the Old Country.

In fact, early accounts suggest that a Christmas without plum pudding was not considered much of a Christmas at all. One settler, a man named John Langton, whose letters describe life on the shore of Sturgeon Lake in Ontario in the 1830s, tried to make plum pudding one Christmas, even though ingredients were scarce. Although it was "a decided failure," he reported that the pudding was eaten anyway.

And Paul Kane, a Canadian artist originally from Ireland, wrote about an unusual Christmas feast in Edmonton in 1847. The First Nations people in the encampment that he was visiting provided him with what appears to be a very elaborate Christmas dinner, consisting of "boiled buffalo hump, boiled buffalo calf, dried moose nose, white fish, buffalo tongue, beavers' tails, roast wild goose, piles of potatoes, turnips and bread." But despite the lavish meal, Kane still lamented that there were no "pies, puddings or blanc manges."

When the necessary ingredients were not to be had, settlers improvised. Apples and pumpkins were substituted for unavailable ingredients, and unusual (and delicious) variations of the old favourites resulted. The recipes in this chapter both reflect the ingenuity of those early settlers and pay homage to some of the traditional desserts they brought with them to their new land.

Plum Pudding

Makes three 1-quart (1 L) puddings or one 3-quart (3 L) pudding; 18 to 24 servings

Plum pudding is best if made 2 to 4 weeks ahead of time and refrigerated until needed. To reheat the pudding, return it to the mould and steam it as described in the recipe for 1½ hours or until heated through.

....

4½ cups (1.12 L) Thompson raisins
2 cups (500 mL) currants
1½ cups (375 mL) diced mixed candied peel
1¼ cups (300 mL) orange juice or brandy
¾ cup (175 mL) chopped candied cherries
1½ cups (375 mL) all-purpose flour
1½ tsp (7 mL) baking powder

1 tsp (5 mL) cinnamon
½ tsp (2 mL) ground allspice
½ tsp (2 mL) ground cloves
½ tsp (2 mL) salt
3 eggs
2 cups (500 mL) lightly packed brown sugar
2 cups (500 mL) finely chopped beef suet** (see note on facing page)
2 cups (500 mL) fine white fresh breadcrumbs

2 tsp (10 mL) grated lemon zest
3 Tbsp (45 mL) fresh lemon juice
2 small apples, cored and chopped but unpeeled
1 cup (250 mL) blanched slivered almonds
¼ cup (60 mL) brandy for flaming (optional)

IN A LARGE GLASS BOWL, combine the raisins, currants, peel, orange juice and cherries. Cover and let sit overnight.

Prepare three 1-quart (1 L) heatproof pudding moulds or bowls, or one 3-quart (3 L) heatproof pudding mould or bowl by greasing them with butter and sprinkling them with granulated sugar.

In a large bowl, sift together the flour, baking powder, spices and salt. Drain the fruit, reserving the liquid. Add the fruit to the flour mixture and combine well.

In a separate large bowl, beat the eggs well. Add the brown sugar and suet and beat together well. Stir in the breadcrumbs. Add the lemon zest, lemon juice and the reserved liquid from the dried fruit. Stir in the fruit-flour mixture, chopped apples and almonds, mixing only to blend.

Scrape the batter into the prepared moulds to no more than three-quarters full. Cover with a double thickness of wax paper and foil and tie securely with string.

Place the moulds on a rack in a very large pot or two smaller pots. Pour boiling water around the moulds to come two-thirds of the way up them. Cover the pot tightly and steam for 3 to 4 hours or until the tops of the puddings are no longer sticky, topping up the pot with more boiling water as necessary. Remove the moulds from the water. Let the puddings set in the moulds for about 5 minutes.

To serve, turn the pudding out onto a warm platter (make sure the platter is heatproof if you are going to flame the pudding). To flame the pudding, warm the brandy in a small saucepan but do not let it boil. Avert your face, ignite the brandy with a match and immediately pour it over the warm pudding, basting the pudding while the brandy flames. Serve hot with Hard Sauce (page 34), Rich Caramel Sauce (page 34) or Creamy Dressing (page 37).

Steamed Cranberry Pudding

Makes two 1-quart (1 L) puddings; 12 servings

Tangy cranberries marry with sweet apricots for
a delicious, moist pudding.

....

2 cups (500 mL) chopped
   fresh or frozen cranberries*
¾ cup (175 mL) chopped
   walnuts
½ cup (125 mL) chopped
   dried apricots

2 cups (500 mL) all-purpose
   flour, divided
1 Tbsp (15 mL) baking powder
1 tsp (5 mL) salt
1 cup (250 mL) fine dry
   breadcrumbs

1 cup (250 mL) finely
   chopped beef suet**
1 cup (250 mL) lightly packed
   brown sugar
2 eggs
⅔ cup (150 mL) milk
1 tsp (5 mL) almond extract

PREPARE TWO 1-quart (1 L) heatproof pudding moulds or bowls by greasing them with butter and sprinkling them with granulated sugar.

Toss the cranberries, walnuts and apricots with ¼ cup (60 mL) of the flour.

In a medium bowl, sift the remaining flour with the baking powder and salt. Add the breadcrumbs.

In a large bowl, beat together the suet, brown sugar and eggs. Add the dry ingredients in three additions, alternating with the milk. Stir in the cranberry mixture and almond extract, mixing well.

Scrape the batter into the prepared moulds to no more than three-quarters full. Cover with a double thickness of wax paper and foil and tie securely with string.

Place the moulds on a rack in a very large pot or two smaller pots. Pour boiling water around the moulds to come two-thirds of the way up them. Cover the pot tightly and steam for 2 to 2½ hours or until the tops of the puddings are no longer sticky, topping up the pot with more boiling water as necessary. Remove the moulds from the water. Let the puddings set in the moulds for about 5 minutes.

To serve, turn the puddings out onto a warm platter and serve hot with Rich Caramel Sauce, Hard Sauce, Almond Sauce or Brandy Hard Sauce (page 34). If you use Brandy Hard Sauce, try substituting 2 Tbsp (30 mL) apricot brandy for the regular brandy.

* If using frozen cranberries, there's no need to thaw them first.

** Suet is the fat that surrounds beef cattle's kidneys. Look for it at the butcher's or in your supermarket's meat freezer.

Steamed Carrot Pudding

Makes one 2-quart (2 L) or two 1-quart (1 L) puddings; 10 to 12 servings

Although the grated vegetables were probably first used as filler
in this German interpretation of plum pudding, they do add a great deal
to the texture and taste of the pudding. This pudding freezes well if
you wrap it in plastic wrap, then put it in an airtight container.
To reheat, thaw the pudding, return it to the mould, cover as before
and steam for 1½ hours or until heated through. Fluffy White Pudding
Sauce (page 35) is particularly good with this pudding.

··

2 cups (500 mL) finely
  chopped beef suet*
1½ cups (375 mL) lightly
  packed brown sugar
1 egg, beaten
1 Tbsp (15 mL) corn syrup
1 cup (250 mL) grated raw
  carrot
1 cup (250 mL) grated raw
  potato
2 cups (500 mL) all-purpose
  flour

1 tsp (5 mL) salt
½ tsp (2 mL) cinnamon
½ tsp (2 mL) ground allspice
⅛ tsp (0.5 mL) freshly grated
  nutmeg
1½ cups (375 mL) mixed
  diced candied peel
1½ cups (375 mL) whole
  candied cherries
1 cup (250 mL) golden
  sultana raisins
1 cup (250 mL) currants

⅔ cup (150 mL) chopped
  candied pineapple
½ cup (125 mL) chopped
  walnuts
1 cup (250 mL) fine dry
  breadcrumbs
1 cup (250 mL) buttermilk**
1 tsp (5 mL) baking soda
2 Tbsp (30 mL) brandy

PREPARE ONE 2-quart (2 L) or two 1-quart
(1 L) heatproof pudding moulds or bowls by
greasing them with butter and sprinkling
them with granulated sugar.

In a large bowl, beat together the suet,
brown sugar, egg and corn syrup. Stir in the
grated carrot and potato.

In a separate large bowl, sift together
the flour, salt, cinnamon, allspice and
nutmeg. Measure ½ cup (125 mL) of the
flour mixture into a medium bowl, add the
candied peel, cherries, raisins, currants,
pineapple and walnuts and toss well.

Add the breadcrumbs to the remaining
dry ingredients.

In a small bowl, stir together the
buttermilk and baking soda.

Add the dry ingredients to the suet
mixture, alternating with the buttermilk

mixture. Stir in the brandy and the peel,
fruit and nuts.

Scrape the batter into the prepared
moulds (the moulds should be no more than
three-quarters full). Cover with a double
thickness of wax paper and foil and tie
securely with string.

Place the moulds on a rack in a very
large pot or on racks in two smaller pots.
Pour boiling water around the moulds to
come two-thirds of the way up the moulds.
Cover the pot tightly and steam for 3 hours
or until the tops of the puddings are no
longer sticky, topping up the pot with more
boiling water as necessary. Remove the
moulds from the water. Let the puddings
set in the moulds for about 5 minutes.

To serve, turn out the puddings onto
a warm platter and serve hot with Fluffy

White Pudding Sauce, Lemon Sauce or Hard Sauce (recipes start on page 34).

* Suet is the fat that surrounds beef cattle's kidneys. Look for it at the butcher's or in your supermarket's meat freezer.

** If buttermilk is unavailable, stir 2 tsp (10 mL) fresh lemon juice or white vinegar into 1 cup (250 mL) milk and let stand for 10 minutes before using.

Steamed Fig Pudding

Makes two 1-quart (1 L) puddings; 12 servings

Empty coffee cans are excellent for small puddings like this one. The recipe fits nicely into three 1-pound (500 g) cans.

....

1 cup (250 mL) dried figs, about 4 oz (125 g)
¾ cup (175 mL) butter, softened
1 cup (250 mL) granulated sugar

2 eggs, beaten
2 cups (500 mL) all-purpose flour
1 tsp (5 mL) baking powder
1 tsp (5 mL) ground mace
1 tsp (5 mL) cinnamon

½ tsp (2 mL) salt
¾ cup (175 mL) orange juice
½ cup (125 mL) blanched slivered almonds
1 tsp (5 mL) vanilla

PREPARE TWO 1-quart (1 L) heatproof pudding moulds or bowls by greasing them with butter and sprinkling them with granulated sugar.

Snip off the stems from the figs, then grind them in a food processor. (Alternatively, mince the figs very finely with a sharp knife. Don't use a blender for this; it will turn the figs to mush.) Set aside.

In a large bowl, cream the butter. Add the sugar and beat until light and fluffy. Beat in the eggs, then stir in the ground figs.

In a medium bowl, sift together the flour, baking powder, spices and salt. Add the dry ingredients to the creamed mixture alternately with the orange juice. Stir in the almonds and vanilla.

Scrape the batter into the prepared moulds (the moulds should be no more than three-quarters full). Cover with a double thickness of wax paper and foil and tie securely with string. Place the moulds on a rack in a very large pot or on racks in two smaller pots. Pour boiling water around the moulds to come two-thirds of the way up the moulds. Cover the pot tightly and steam for 2½ to 3 hours or until the tops of the puddings are no longer sticky, topping up the pot with more boiling water as necessary. Remove the moulds from the water. Let the puddings set in the moulds for about 5 minutes.

To serve, turn out the puddings onto a warm platter and serve hot with Foamy Orange Sauce or Rich Caramel Sauce (recipes start on page 34).

Cranberry Sherbet

Makes 8 servings

Serve this refreshing ice at the end of a heavy meal or between two rich courses as a light interlude to refresh the palate.

....

4 cups (1 L) fresh or frozen cranberries*

2 cups (500 mL) water

1 envelope (1 Tbsp/15 mL) unflavoured gelatin

1 cup (250 mL) cold fruity white wine, such as Riesling, or cold water

2 cups (500 mL) granulated sugar

2 tsp (10 mL) grated lemon zest

3 Tbsp (45 mL) fresh lemon juice

IN A LARGE SAUCEPAN, combine the cranberries and water. Boil for about 5 minutes or until the skins pop.

Meanwhile, in a small bowl, sprinkle the gelatin over the wine and let it stand for 5 minutes to soften.

Purée the cranberries in a food processor or blender, then rub them through a sieve, discarding the skins. Return the cranberry purée to the saucepan. Add the sugar and softened gelatin mixture. Cook, stirring, over medium heat until the sugar and gelatin dissolve.

Remove from the heat and let cool. Stir in the lemon zest and juice. Pour into a shallow 4- to 6-cup (2 to 2.5 L) metal pan, cover with foil and place in the freezer. Freeze for 3 hours, until firm.

Scrape the frozen mixture out into a chilled bowl and beat with an electric mixer until slushy. Return the sherbet to the metal pan, cover and freeze for at least 3 hours until firm, stirring two or three times.

* If using frozen cranberries, there's no need to thaw them first.

Creamy Cranberry Mousse

Makes 8 to 10 servings

This smooth, creamy dessert can be made days before a dinner party. Served with a plate of Christmas cookies, it's a light, refreshing way to end a hearty holiday dinner.

....

1 cup (250 mL) fresh or frozen cranberries*
½ cup (125 mL) water
1½ cups (375 mL) granulated sugar, divided
2 Tbsp (30 mL) grated orange zest

½ cup (125 mL) cold orange juice
1 envelope (1 Tbsp/15 mL) unflavoured gelatin
4 eggs, separated
1 cup (250 mL) whipping (35%) cream

Additional sweetened whipped cream
Red and green candied cherries

IN A MEDIUM SAUCEPAN, combine the cranberries and water. Boil for about 5 minutes or until the skins pop. Purée the cooked cranberries in a food processor or blender, then rub them through a sieve, discarding the skins. Add 1 cup (250 mL) of the sugar and the grated orange zest to the warm cranberry purée and stir until the sugar has dissolved. Cool.

In the top half of a double boiler or in a heatproof bowl, combine the cold orange juice and gelatin and let sit for 5 minutes. Place the top half of the double boiler or heatproof bowl over a saucepan of simmering water and heat until warm, stirring often.

Meanwhile, in a medium bowl, beat the egg yolks together until blended. Gradually stir in 2 Tbsp (30 mL) of the warm orange juice mixture. Slowly pour the egg yolk mixture into the warm orange juice mixture, stirring constantly. Continue to stir over simmering water for about 4 minutes or until thickened. Remove

from the simmering water, lay a piece of buttered wax paper directly on the surface of the orange mixture and cool to room temperature.

In a large bowl with clean beaters, beat the egg whites until foamy. Gradually add the remaining sugar and continue beating until stiff but still moist.

In a separate large bowl, whip the cream until soft peaks form. Fold the cranberry purée, orange mixture, then the egg whites into the whipped cream. Spoon into a large serving bowl, cover and place in the freezer for 2 to 3 hours before serving. The mousse can be frozen for up to 3 days, in which case remove it from the freezer 30 minutes before serving.

Just before serving, garnish the mousse with whipped cream and pieces of red and green candied cherries.

* If using frozen cranberries, there's no need to thaw them first.

Mincemeat Trifle

Makes 12 servings

Trifle is an elegant dessert that originated in Britain. Although sensational in appearance and taste, it is quite simple to make. You'll need half of the Old-Fashioned Pound Cake (page 14) for this.

....

CUSTARD
4 egg yolks
¼ cup (60 mL) granulated sugar
2 cups (500 mL) half-and-half (10%) or table (18%) cream
1½ tsp (7 mL) vanilla

TRIFLE
½ Old-Fashioned Pound Cake (page 14)
⅓ cup (75 mL) dry sherry
2 cups (500 mL) Mincemeat (page 41)

1¼ cups (300 mL) whipping (35%) cream
¼ cup (60 mL) icing sugar
½ tsp (2 mL) vanilla
Angelica, candied peel or candied cherries for garnish

TO MAKE THE CUSTARD, in a medium bowl, beat the egg yolks with the granulated sugar until thick. Heat the cream in the top half of a double boiler or in a heatproof bowl set over a saucepan of simmering water.

Stirring constantly, pour the warm cream slowly into the beaten egg yolks, then return the whole mixture to the top half of the double boiler or the heatproof bowl. Stirring constantly, cook over simmering water for about 4 minutes until the custard thickly coats a spoon.

Remove from the heat and stir in the vanilla. Pour the custard into a clean bowl and lay a piece of buttered wax paper directly on the surface of the custard. Chill for at least 3 hours.

To make the trifle, spread a thin layer of chilled custard in the bottom of a large glass serving bowl or glass baking dish.

Cut the pound cake into ½-inch (1 cm) slices, then cut the slices into strips. Put half of the cake strips on top of the custard in the bowl and sprinkle with half of the sherry. Spread half of the mincemeat over the cake. Pour 1 cup (250 mL) of the custard over the mincemeat. Repeat with the remaining cake, sherry, mincemeat and custard. Cover and chill overnight.

Just before serving, whip the cream until soft peaks form. Whip in the icing sugar and vanilla. Smooth half of the whipped cream on top of the trifle. Using a pastry bag, pipe the remaining whipped cream in rosettes around the edge. If you don't have a pastry bag, spoon all of the cream over the trifle and make decorative swirls with a knife. Garnish with strips of angelica, candied peel or bits of candied cherries.

RASPBERRY OR STRAWBERRY TRIFLE
Follow the recipe for Mincemeat Trifle, substituting two thawed and drained 10 oz (283 g) packages of frozen unsweetened raspberries or strawberries and 1 cup (250 mL) slivered almonds or coarsely chopped walnuts for the mincemeat. Reserve a few whole raspberries and some of the almonds for the garnish.

Apple Snow with Custard Sauce

Makes 6 to 8 servings

Here's an easy dessert that makes good use of any late-fall apples
you may still have in your fridge or fruit bowl. Prep this frothy dessert
early in the day for an evening dinner party.

···

APPLE SNOW
4 medium-sized red apples,
   cored and quartered but
   unpeeled
¾ cup (175 mL) water, divided
1 envelope (1 Tbsp/15 mL)
   unflavoured gelatin
½ cup (125 mL) apple cider
½ cup (125 mL) firmly packed
   brown sugar

2 tsp (10 mL) grated lemon
   zest
3 Tbsp (45 mL) fresh lemon
   juice
Freshly grated nutmeg to
   taste
3 egg whites

CUSTARD SAUCE
½ cup (125 mL) milk
¼ cup (60 mL) granulated
   sugar
⅛ tsp (0.5 mL) salt
3 egg yolks
2 Tbsp (30 mL) apple brandy,
   such as Calvados
⅓ cup (75 mL) whipping
   (35%) cream

TO MAKE THE APPLE SNOW, combine the
apples and ½ cup (125 mL) of the water in
a medium saucepan. Cook over medium
heat for 10 minutes or until soft. Purée
the cooked apples in a food processor
or blender, then rub through a sieve,
discarding the peel. Set aside.

Meanwhile, in a small saucepan, soften
the gelatin in the remaining water. Allow to
stand for 5 minutes. Add the cider and stir
over low heat until the gelatin has dissolved.
Remove from the heat and stir in the brown
sugar, lemon zest, lemon juice and nutmeg
to taste. Scrape into a medium bowl. Chill
until slightly thickened, 30 to 45 minutes,
then beat until frothy.

In a medium bowl, beat the egg whites
until stiff but still moist. Fold the beaten
egg whites and apple purée into the gelatin
mixture. Cover and chill for 2 hours or
until set.

To make the custard sauce, in a small
saucepan, bring the milk, granulated sugar
and salt just to a simmer.

In a small bowl, beat the egg yolks
slightly and gradually stir in the warm
milk. Pour the mixture into the top half of
a double boiler or a heatproof bowl set over
a saucepan of simmering water and cook
over low heat, stirring constantly, for about
4 minutes, until the custard is thick enough
to coat a spoon. Remove from the heat, cool
and stir in the apple brandy. Chill.

Just before serving, whip the cream in
a small bowl until stiff peaks form, then
fold it into the custard sauce. Divide the
apple snow among 6 or 8 dessert glasses and
spoon some of the custard sauce overtop
each serving.

Cranberry-Glazed Cheesecake

Makes 12 servings

Cheesecake is always a favourite of both eaters and cooks (since it can be made ahead). The colourful cranberry glaze makes this one a lovely addition to any holiday table.

....

CRUST

1 cup (250 mL) all-purpose flour

¼ cup (60 mL) granulated sugar

1 tsp (5 mL) grated lemon zest

¼ cup (60 mL) butter, softened

1 egg yolk

½ tsp (2 mL) vanilla

FILLING

5 eggs, separated

¼ cup (60 mL) plus ⅔ cup (150 mL) granulated sugar, divided

2 pkgs (250 g each) block cream cheese

1 cup (250 mL) sour cream

¼ cup (60 mL) all-purpose flour

1 Tbsp (15 mL) grated lemon zest

3 Tbsp (45 mL) fresh lemon juice

1 tsp (5 mL) vanilla

TOPPING

¾ cup (175 mL) granulated sugar

1 envelope (1 Tbsp/15 mL) unflavoured gelatin

¾ cup (175 mL) water

2 cups (500 mL) fresh or frozen cranberries*

1 tsp (5 mL) grated lemon zest

2 Tbsp (30 mL) fresh lemon juice

LIGHTLY GREASE A 9-inch (2.5 L) springform pan. Preheat the oven to 325°F (160°C).

To make the crust, in a medium bowl, combine the flour, sugar and lemon zest. Make a well in the centre of the dry ingredients and in it place the butter, egg yolk and vanilla. Blend with a fork, then mix with your fingers until the dough starts to hold together. It will be fairly crumbly. Press evenly over the bottom and partway up the sides of the prepared pan.

To make the filling, in a large bowl, beat the egg whites until stiff but still moist. Gradually beat in ¼ cup (60 mL) of the sugar until stiff and shiny. Set aside.

In a separate large bowl, cream the cream cheese until softened. Beat in the egg yolks, one at a time. Gradually beat in the remaining sugar, the sour cream, flour,

lemon zest, lemon juice and vanilla. Fold in the stiff egg whites.

Pour the cream cheese mixture into the prepared pan. Bake for 1¼ hours or until almost set. Cool for 10 minutes, then run a metal spatula carefully around the edge to loosen it. Cool completely.

To make the topping, combine the sugar and gelatin in a small saucepan. Gradually add the water. Slowly bring to a boil, stirring often. Add the cranberries, lemon zest and juice. Cook, stirring, for about 5 minutes until the cranberries pop.

Remove from the heat and let cool slightly, then refrigerate until the mixture begins to thicken, stirring occasionally.

With a metal spatula, loosen the pan sides from the cooled cheesecake and remove them. Loosen the cheesecake from the bottom of the pan with a spatula and carefully slide it onto a serving plate.

Pour the cranberry mixture over the cheesecake, spreading it over the top. Refrigerate for about 3 hours until the topping is set. If the cheesecake has been refrigerated for longer, remove it from the refrigerator 45 minutes to 1 hour before serving for a creamier texture.

* If using frozen cranberries, there's no need to thaw them first.

Winter Fruit Salad

Makes 15 servings

This fruit salad should be made a few hours or—better still—
a day ahead of time so that the flavours can mingle. Serve it chilled,
with or without Creamy Dressing (page 37), as a refreshing start to
a brunch or as a light dessert after a rich meal.

1 lemon
5 oranges
1 cup (250 mL) water
¾ cup (175 mL) granulated
  sugar

¼ cup (60 mL) orange liqueur
1 pink grapefruit
3 firm winter pears
3 Red Delicious apples
2 bananas

2 cups (500 mL) halved
  seedless red grapes
1 pkg (10 oz/283 g) frozen
  unsweetened strawberries
  or raspberries

SQUEEZE THE JUICE from the lemon and 2 of the oranges into a small saucepan. Add the water and sugar. Stir over medium heat until the sugar has dissolved. Bring to a boil and boil, uncovered, for 5 minutes. Remove from the heat and cool. Add the liqueur.

Peel and remove the white membrane from the 3 remaining oranges and the grapefruit. Cut the citrus fruit into 2-inch (5 cm) chunks.

Core the pears and apples, leaving the skin on. Cut them into 2-inch (5 cm) chunks. Peel and thickly slice the bananas. Put the prepared fruit and grapes in a large glass serving bowl. Pour in the sugar syrup and mix gently. Cover and chill.

Thaw the strawberries or raspberries just until the fruit separates. Add them to the fruit salad 30 minutes before serving.

Hard Sauce

Makes about 1¼ cups (300 mL)

This thick sauce is delicious with Steamed Cranberry Pudding
(page 25) or Plum Pudding (page 24).

....

¼ cup (60 mL) butter,
softened

1 cup (250 mL) icing sugar
1 tsp (5 mL) lemon extract

1 egg white

IN A MEDIUM BOWL, cream the butter until very light. Gradually add the icing sugar and continue to cream until fluffy. Gradually add the lemon extract.

In a separate medium bowl, beat the egg white until stiff, then fold it into the butter and sugar mixture. Spoon into a small serving dish and chill until firm.

ALMOND SAUCE Follow the recipe for Hard Sauce, substituting ½ tsp (2 mL) almond extract for the lemon extract. This sauce is excellent with steamed Cranberry Pudding.

BRANDY HARD SAUCE Follow the recipe for Hard Sauce, omitting the egg white and substituting 2 Tbsp (30 mL) brandy for the lemon extract. You can also add 1 tsp (5 mL) vanilla, if you like.

Rich Caramel Sauce

Makes about 2 cups (500 mL)

This rich, sticky sauce is good with most steamed puddings.

....

1 cup (250 mL) firmly packed
brown sugar
1½ tsp (7 mL) cornstarch

1 cup (250 mL) half-and-
half (10%) or table (18%)
cream

¼ cup (60 mL) butter
2 Tbsp (30 mL) brandy
1 tsp (5 mL) vanilla

COMBINE THE BROWN SUGAR and cornstarch in the top half of a double boiler or in a heatproof bowl. Gradually add the cream and stir until the sugar is dissolved.

Place the top half of the double boiler or the bowl over simmering water. Add the butter and cook, stirring constantly, until the mixture is smooth and thickens slightly. Continue to cook for 10 minutes, stirring often.

Remove from the heat and stir in the brandy and vanilla. Serve hot over any hot steamed pudding.

Fluffy White Pudding Sauce

Makes about 3 cups (750 mL)

This beautifully creamy sauce complements any steamed pudding.
It is also delicious with hot mincemeat tarts.

½ cup (125 mL) butter,
softened
2 eggs, separated
1 cup (250 mL) granulated
sugar

¼ cup (60 mL) all-purpose
flour
1 cup (250 mL) milk
1 cup (250 mL) whipping
(35%) cream

1 tsp (5 mL) vanilla
Pinch of freshly grated
nutmeg

COMBINE THE BUTTER and egg yolks in the top half of a double boiler or in a heatproof bowl set over a saucepan of simmering water. Add the sugar and flour and blend well. Gradually stir in the milk.

Cook over simmering water for about 10 minutes, stirring constantly, until the mixture is like a thin custard. Remove from the simmering water and let cool.

In a medium bowl, beat the egg whites until stiff. In a separate medium bowl, whip the cream until stiff peaks form. When the sauce is cool, add the vanilla, then carefully fold in the whipped cream and egg whites. Refrigerate until needed. (The sauce can be made a day in advance, if necessary.) Top with a light sprinkling of freshly grated nutmeg before serving.

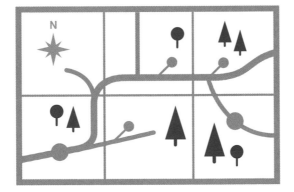

Lemon Sauce

Makes about 3 cups (750 mL)

Rich with the flavour of lemon, this clear, thin sauce is
delicious with Steamed Carrot Pudding (page 26) or
Steamed Cranberry Pudding (page 25).

1 cup (250 mL) granulated
  sugar
2 Tbsp (30 mL) cornstarch
¼ tsp (1 mL) salt

2 cups (500 mL) boiling
  water
3 Tbsp (45 mL) butter

½ tsp (2 mL) grated lemon
  zest
3 Tbsp (45 mL) fresh lemon
  juice

COMBINE THE SUGAR, cornstarch and
salt in the top half of a double boiler or
in a heatproof bowl set over a saucepan of
simmering water. Slowly add the boiling
water to the sugar mixture, stirring
constantly. Cook over simmering water for
15 minutes, or until the sauce becomes clear
and thickens slightly.

When ready to serve, remove from the
heat and add the butter, lemon zest and
juice, stirring until the butter melts. Serve
hot.

Foamy Orange Sauce

Makes about 1½ cups (375 mL)

This sauce goes particularly well with Steamed Fig Pudding (page 27).
....

½ cup (125 mL) butter,
   softened
1 cup (250 mL) icing sugar

1 egg, beaten
2 Tbsp (30 mL) orange juice

1 tsp (5 mL) finely grated
   orange zest

IN A MEDIUM BOWL, cream the butter, add the sugar and beat until light and fluffy. Beat in the egg.

Very gradually beat in the orange juice, a drop at a time. Stir in the orange zest. Beat the sauce until light and fluffy. Serve immediately.

Creamy Dressing

Makes about 2 cups (500 mL)

This is good with most steamed puddings and with
Winter Fruit Salad (page 33).
....

1 Tbsp (15 mL) all-purpose
   flour
⅓ cup (75 mL) granulated
   sugar
1 egg

⅓ cup (75 mL) dry white wine
¼ cup (60 mL) orange juice,
   strained
2 Tbsp (30 mL) orange
   liqueur

1 Tbsp (15 mL) fresh lemon
   juice, strained
½ cup (125 mL) whipping
   (35%) cream

COMBINE THE FLOUR and sugar in the top half of a double boiler or in a heatproof bowl set over a saucepan of simmering water. In a small bowl, beat the egg until foamy and add to the flour mixture. Stirring constantly, gradually add the wine, orange juice, liqueur and lemon juice to the flour mixture.

Cook, stirring, over simmering water for 10 minutes or until thickened. Remove from the heat and let cool.

In a medium bowl, whip the cream until stiff peaks form, then fold the cream into the cooled dressing.

Pies and Tarts

ies and tarts have long been part of our Canadian culinary tradition, and the holiday season brings out some of our best. Before candied fruits and such appeared often on grocery shelves, cooks relied on stored produce like pumpkins or green tomatoes, as well as maple syrup for Christmas pies. As soon as raisins and fruit became more common, what British settler could resist making a big batch of mincemeat? Mincemeat pies and tarts remain a favourite, as does the savoury French-Canadian tourtière.

Pie Pastry

Makes enough for three 9-inch (23 cm) double-crust pies or six 9-inch (23 cm) pie shells

Sometimes called Never-Fail Pastry, this recipe yields a good,
tender pastry. Work gently and quickly for best results.

4 cups (1 L) cake-and-pastry
flour
2 cups (500 mL) all-purpose
flour

1½ tsp (7 mL) salt
1 lb (500 g) cold lard
1 egg

1 tsp (5 mL) white vinegar
Cold water

MIX BOTH THE FLOURS and salt together in a large bowl. Cut in the lard with a pastry blender or two knives until the mixture resembles coarse rolled oats.

Put the egg and vinegar in a 1-cup (250 mL) measure and top up to the 1-cup (250 mL) mark with cold water. Stir well.

Add the liquid a bit at a time to the dry mixture, blending it in lightly with a fork.

Finish by combining the two mixtures gently with your hands. The dough may crumble slightly at this point.

Wrap the dough in wax paper or plastic wrap and refrigerate for several hours or overnight to make the pastry easier to work with and more tender. Remove from the refrigerator 30 minutes before rolling.

Mincemeat

Makes about 10 cups (2.5 L)

Traditional English mincemeat is made by allowing the ingredients
to steep for a month in Madeira, rum or brandy. The process is
speeded up in this recipe by cooking the ingredients, then adding
the spirit. Mincemeat improves with age, so make it well in advance
of the holiday season.

You'll need about 4 cups (1 L) mincemeat for a 9- or 10-inch
(23 or 25 cm) pie. Add ¼ cup (60 mL) brandy to the filling if desired.
Once the pie is assembled, bake it at 450°F (230°C) for 10 minutes,
then reduce the temperature to 350°F (180°C) and bake for another
30 minutes or until golden brown.

....

1 cup (250 mL) apple cider
3 medium apples, peeled,
 cored and quartered
4 cups (1 L) finely chopped
 beef suet*
3 cups (750 mL) currants
3 cups (750 mL) Thompson
 raisins
2¼ cups (550 mL) firmly
 packed brown sugar
2¼ cups (550 mL) diced
 mixed candied peel

¾ cup (175 mL) diced mixed
 candied fruit
1 cup (250 mL) chopped
 walnuts
1 cup (250 mL) rum or brandy
2 tsp (10 mL) grated lemon
 zest
3 Tbsp (45 mL) fresh lemon
 juice
1 tsp (5 mL) ground mace

1 tsp (5 mL) cinnamon
1 tsp (5 mL) ground cloves
1 tsp (5 mL) freshly grated
 nutmeg
1 tsp (5 mL) ground coriander
 or ground allspice
½ tsp (2 mL) salt

IN A LARGE heavy-bottomed saucepan,
boil the cider for about 5 minutes. Add the
apples and cook until soft. Remove from the
heat and mash the apples until smooth.

Add the suet, currants, raisins, sugar,
candied peel and candied fruit. Return to
low heat and cook, stirring often, for
1 hour. Add the remaining ingredients
and stir well.

Remove from the heat and let cool
completely. Spoon the mincemeat into
airtight containers and refrigerate for up to
2 weeks, or freeze for up to 1 year.

* Suet is the fat that surrounds beef cattle's
kidneys. Look for it at the butcher's or in
your supermarket's meat freezer.

Green Tomato and Apple Mincemeat

Makes 8 to 12 cups (2 to 3 L)

Turn your late-fall tomatoes into this beautiful mincemeat.
You'll need about 4 cups (1 L) mincemeat for a 9- or 10-inch (23 or 25 cm)
pie. Add 1 cup (250 mL) sliced apples to the filling and ¼ cup (60 mL)
brandy, if desired. Once the pie is assembled, bake it at 450°F (230°C) for
10 minutes, then reduce the temperature to 350°F (180°C) and bake for
another 30 minutes or until golden brown.

....

8 cups (2 L) cored, chopped green tomatoes

1 Tbsp (15 mL) coarse pickling salt

1 large orange, coarsely chopped

10 cups (2.5 L) peeled, cored and chopped apples

3½ cups (875 mL) firmly packed brown sugar

3 cups (750 mL) golden sultana raisins

1½ cups (375 mL) finely chopped beef suet*

1½ cups (375 mL) halved candied cherries (optional)

½ cup (125 mL) diced candied citron peel (optional)

½ cup (125 mL) cider vinegar

2 tsp (10 mL) cinnamon

1 tsp (5 mL) freshly grated nutmeg

½ tsp (2 mL) ground cloves

½ tsp (2 mL) ground allspice

½ tsp (2 mL) ground ginger

½ cup (125 mL) brandy or rum (optional)

IN A LARGE non-reactive pot, combine the tomatoes and salt and let stand for 1 hour.

Drain thoroughly and return the tomatoes to the pot. Add enough boiling water to cover them and let stand for 5 minutes. Drain off the water. Return the tomatoes to the pot.

In a food processor, process the orange until finely minced. (Alternatively, mince the orange very finely with a sharp knife. Don't use a blender for this; it will turn the orange to mush.) Add the orange to the tomatoes, along with the remaining ingredients, except the brandy or rum.

Bring to a boil over high heat, then reduce the heat to medium and cook, uncovered and stirring often, for 35 to 40 minutes, until thickened. Stir in the brandy or rum.

Remove from the heat and let cool completely. Spoon the mincemeat into airtight containers and refrigerate for up to 2 weeks, or freeze for up to 1 year.

* Suet is the fat that surrounds beef cattle's kidneys. Look for it at the butcher's or in your supermarket's meat freezer.

Winter Pie

Makes 5 to 6 servings

Pioneer women probably put together the ingredients for this very
old recipe when they did not have everything they needed to make
mincemeat. Whatever its origins, it is well worth making.

....

1 cup (250 mL) golden
  sultana raisins
½ cup (125 mL) well-packed
  finely grated carrot
½ cup (125 mL) granulated
  sugar
1 Tbsp (15 mL) cornstarch
½ tsp (2 mL) cinnamon

¼ tsp (1 mL) ground cloves
¼ tsp (1 mL) freshly grated
  nutmeg
¼ tsp (1 mL) salt
½ cup (125 mL) hot water
¼ cup (60 mL) apple juice or
  cider

1 cup (250 mL) peeled, cored
  and coarsely chopped
  apple
Pastry for a double-crust
  8-inch (20 cm) pie
  (page 40)

IN A LARGE non-reactive saucepan, combine
the raisins, carrot, sugar, cornstarch, spices
and salt. Stir in the hot water and apple
juice. Bring to a boil over high heat, then
reduce the heat to medium-low and simmer
for about 5 minutes.
Add the apple and simmer for another
15 minutes. Cool.

Preheat the oven to 450°F (230°C). On
a lightly floured surface, roll out half of the
pastry and use it to line an 8-inch (20 cm)
pie plate. Spoon the filling into the bottom
crust, heaping it up slightly in the middle.

Roll out the remaining pastry. Moisten
the pastry on the rim of the pie plate with
cold water, cover with the top crust and
trim and flute the edges firmly. Slash a few
holes near the centre of the pie crust to
allow steam to escape.

Bake for 10 minutes, then reduce the
temperature to 350°F (180°C) and bake for
another 20 minutes or until the pastry is
golden brown.

Pumpkin Pie

Makes 6 servings

Pumpkin pie was often served at pioneer Christmas dinners
because many families still had fresh-looking pumpkins in
their root cellars in December. This recipe makes a particularly
light and very delicious pumpkin pie.

....

1 cup (250 mL) evaporated
milk
2 eggs, separated
¾ cup (175 mL) firmly packed
brown sugar
¼ tsp (1 mL) salt
1 cup (250 mL) pumpkin
purée (not pumpkin-pie
filling)

1 tsp (5 mL) cinnamon
½ tsp (2 mL) ground ginger
½ tsp (2 mL) ground allspice
¼ tsp (1 mL) ground cloves
Freshly grated nutmeg to
taste

Pastry for a single-crust
9-inch (23 cm) pie
(page 40)
Sweetened whipped cream
and sliced candied ginger
for garnish

PREHEAT THE OVEN to 425°F (220°C).

In the top half of a double boiler or in
a heatproof bowl set over a saucepan of
simmering water, heat the milk until just
simmering.

In a medium bowl, beat the egg yolks
slightly. Pour the hot milk into the yolks,
stirring constantly. Add the brown sugar
and salt and return the mixture to the top
half of the double boiler or to the heatproof
bowl. Cook, stirring constantly, for about
4 minutes until the mixture coats a spoon.
Remove from the simmering water.

In a small bowl, stir together the
pumpkin purée and the spices, then fold the
purée into the milk mixture.

In a medium bowl, beat the egg whites
until stiff but still moist, then fold them
into the pumpkin mixture.

On a lightly floured surface, roll out the
pastry and use to line a 9-inch (23 cm) pie
plate. Pour the pumpkin mixture into the
pie shell. Bake for 15 minutes, then reduce
the temperature to 350°F (180°C) and bake
for another 35 to 40 minutes or until the
filling is set. Cool.

Just before serving, pipe sweetened
whipped cream on top of the pie and
garnish with slivers of candied ginger.

Cranberry Pie

Makes 6 to 8 servings

Also called Mock Cherry Pie, this was an old favourite
at Christmas in many Canadian homes.

....

3 cups (750 mL) coarsely
   chopped fresh or frozen
   cranberries*
1 cup (250 mL) lightly packed
   brown sugar

2 Tbsp (30 mL) water
1 tsp (5 mL) almond extract
Pastry for a double-crust
   9-inch (23 cm) pie
   (page 40)

1 Tbsp (15 mL) quick-cooking
   tapioca
2 Tbsp (30 mL) butter

PREHEAT THE OVEN to 450°F (230°C).

In a medium bowl, stir together the cranberries, brown sugar, water and almond extract.

On a lightly floured surface, roll out half of the pastry and use to line a 9-inch (23 cm) pie plate. Sprinkle half of the tapioca over the bottom. Pour in the cranberry mixture. Sprinkle with the remaining tapioca and dot with butter.

Roll out the remaining pastry and cut into ¾-inch (2 cm) strips. Moisten the pastry on the rim of the pie with cold water. Cover the pie with the pastry strips, weaving them to make a lattice and sealing them to the edge of the pie.

Bake for 10 minutes then reduce the temperature to 350°F (180°C) and bake for another 30 minutes or until the crust is golden brown. Serve warm or at room temperature with sweetened whipped cream or vanilla ice cream.

* If using frozen cranberries, there's no need to thaw them first.

Maple Sugar Pie

Makes 6 to 8 servings

Among French Canadians, two popular desserts for the holidays
are Maple Syrup Pie (facing page) and this one, Maple Sugar Pie from
New Brunswick, which is not as rich or sweet as its name suggests.

....

2 cups (500 mL) maple sugar
1 cup (250 mL) water
1 cup (250 mL) whipping
   (35%) cream
6 Tbsp (90 mL) butter

6 Tbsp (90 mL) all-purpose
   flour
½ cup (125 mL) chopped
   walnuts

Pastry for a single-crust
   9-inch (23 cm) pie
   (page 40)
Whipped cream (optional)

IN A MEDIUM SAUCEPAN, combine the
maple sugar and water. Bring to a boil over
high heat, then reduce the heat to medium-
low and simmer for 10 minutes. Add
the cream and simmer over low heat for
5 minutes, stirring constantly. Remove from
the heat.

In a small saucepan, melt the butter over
low heat. Add the flour and stir over low
heat for 5 minutes. Do not brown. Add the
butter mixture to the maple sugar mixture
and cook, stirring, over medium-low heat

for another 15 minutes or until thickened.
Remove from the heat and add the chopped
nuts. Cool.

Preheat the oven to 450°F (230°C). On
a lightly floured surface, roll out the pastry
and use to line a 9-inch (23 cm) pie plate.
Pour the filling into the crust.

Bake for 10 minutes, then reduce the
temperature to 350°F (180°C) and bake
for another 30 minutes. Serve at room
temperature with whipped cream, if
desired.

Maple Syrup Pie

Makes 6 to 8 servings

If you prefer, spoon the filling for this pie into 12 tiny uncooked tart shells
and bake for about 20 minutes at 375°F (190°C). Cover the tarts with
meringue, then follow the instructions for browning them.

....

FILLING
1 cup (250 mL) maple syrup
½ cup (125 mL) plus 3 Tbsp
  (45 mL) water, divided
¼ cup (60 mL) cornstarch
¼ cup (60 mL) chopped
  walnuts

¼ cup (60 mL) butter
½ tsp (2 mL) vanilla
Pastry for an 8-inch (20 cm)
  shallow flan pan (page 40)

MERINGUE
2 egg whites

½ tsp (2 mL) cream of tartar
¼ cup (60 mL) granulated
  sugar
2 Tbsp (30 mL) water
½ tsp (2 mL) vanilla
⅛ tsp (0.5 mL) salt

TO MAKE THE FILLING, boil the maple syrup and ½ cup (125 mL) of the water together in a small saucepan for 5 minutes.

In a small bowl, stir together the cornstarch and the remaining water until smooth. Add slowly to the boiling liquid, stirring constantly. Cook, stirring, for about 10 minutes, until the mixture is smooth and thick. Remove from the heat. Stir in the walnuts, butter and vanilla. Cool.

Preheat the oven to 450°F (230°C). On a lightly floured surface, roll out the pastry and use to line an 8-inch (20 cm) shallow flan pan. Pour the filling into the crust and bake for 10 minutes. Reduce the temperature to 350°F (180°C) and bake for another 30 minutes or until the filling is firm.

Remove the pie from the oven and increase the temperature to 375°F (190°C).

To make the meringue, beat the egg whites and cream of tartar together in a large bowl until moist peaks form. Very gradually beat in the sugar. Add the remaining ingredients and beat until stiff and shiny.

Spread the meringue over the filling, making sure the meringue touches the pastry rim all the way around. Swirl the meringue into decorative peaks and bake for 12 to 15 minutes or until the tips of the meringue are golden. Remove from the oven and let cool slowly.

Frozen Mincemeat Cream Tarts

Makes 24 tarts

Serve these for an open-house party, or have them on hand
for drop-in guests over the holidays.

....

1 cup (250 mL) whipping (35%) cream
1 cup (250 mL) sour cream

¼ cup (60 mL) dark rum
1 cup (250 mL) Mincemeat (page 41)

24 baked 2-inch (5 cm) tart shells
Whipped cream

IN A MEDIUM BOWL, whip the cream until stiff peaks form. Fold in the sour cream and dark rum. Fold in the mincemeat.

Spoon the cream mixture into tart shells and freeze for 3 to 4 hours or until firm.

Fifteen minutes before serving, remove the tarts from the freezer and top each one with a dab of whipped cream.

Lemon Butter

Makes enough filling for about eighteen 2-inch (5 cm) tart shells

Popular as a filling for tiny tarts at Christmas, lemon butter
is sometimes called lemon cheese or lemon curd. Spoon it into baked
tart shells just before serving and top with whipped cream.
Lemon butter keeps well in a jar stored in the refrigerator and
is also delicious as a cake filling or a spread for toast.

....

3 eggs
1 cup (250 mL) granulated sugar

⅓ cup (75 mL) butter
2 tsp (10 mL) grated lemon zest

⅓ cup (75 mL) fresh lemon juice

IN THE TOP HALF of a double boiler or in a heatproof bowl set over a saucepan of simmering water, beat the eggs slightly. Stir in the sugar, butter, lemon zest and lemon juice. Cook, stirring constantly, over simmering water until the mixture resembles runny custard. (It will thicken a little as it cools.) Remove from the simmering water and let cool. Chill before using.

Tourtière

Makes 6 servings

This French-Canadian meat pie is traditionally served for Christmas Eve dinner. There is a story that the name originated in the 16th century when tourtes, large wild pigeons, abounded in New France. Settlers felled the birds by the thousands and thrifty housewives transformed them into a variety of meat pies, including tarte à la tourte, now abbreviated to tourtière. Others say its name can be traced back to the cast-iron pan of the same name brought to New France by settlers in the 17th century.

....

1 medium potato
1 lb (500 g) lean ground pork
1 medium onion, chopped
1 stalk celery, cut in 3 pieces
1 clove garlic, minced
½ tsp (2 mL) salt
½ tsp (2 mL) crumbled dried sage

½ tsp (2 mL) dried thyme leaves
⅛ tsp (0.5 mL) ground cloves
Freshly ground black pepper to taste
Pastry for a double-crust 9-inch (23 cm) pie (page 40)

1 egg, beaten
1 Tbsp (15 mL) water
Chili sauce or green tomato relish to serve

IN A MEDIUM SAUCEPAN, cook the potato in boiling water for 30 minutes or until tender. Reserving the water, drain well. Mash the potato and set aside.

Return ½ cup (125 mL) of the reserved water to the saucepan (discarding the rest) and bring to a boil. Add the pork, vegetables, salt, herbs and spices. Simmer, uncovered, over medium heat for about 45 minutes or until the pork has lost its pink colour and the liquid has reduced by half. Remove and discard the celery. Stir in the mashed potato and let the mixture cool.

Preheat the oven to 450°F (230°C). On a lightly floured surface, roll out half of the pastry and use it to line a 9-inch (23 cm) pie plate.

Skim off any excess fat from the surface of the potato and meat mixture and spoon the filling into the pie shell. Roll out the remaining pastry. Moisten the pastry on the rim of the pie plate with cold water, cover with the top crust and trim and flute the edges firmly. Slash a few holes near the centre of the pie crust to allow steam to escape. In a small bowl, combine the beaten egg with the water and brush over the top crust.

Bake for 10 minutes, then reduce the temperature to 350°F (180°C) and bake for another 20 minutes or until the crust is golden. Serve hot with chili sauce or green tomato relish. Tourtières freeze well. Thaw in the refrigerator overnight, then cover loosely with foil and reheat in a 350°F (180°C) oven for 30 minutes or until a knife inserted into one of the steam vents for 15 seconds comes out hot.

Acadian Meat Pie

Makes 12 to 14 servings

This six-layer meat pie goes by many names—cipâte, six-pâtes, cipaille, si-paille, sea-pie, pâté en pâté are just a few. And there are just as many recipes for it as names, using a wide range and combination of meat, such as rabbit, venison, moose, partridge or other wild birds, chicken, pork, veal, beef, turkey, lamb, duck and goose.

....

FILLING
3 lb (1.5 kg) whole chicken
3 lb (1.5 kg) whole rabbit
2 lb (1 kg) lean boneless pork
2 lb (1 kg) boneless stewing beef
2 large onions, chopped
1½ cups (375 mL) diced celery
1 cup (250 mL) thinly sliced carrots
2 tsp (10 mL) salt
½ tsp (2 mL) freshly ground black pepper
½ tsp (2 mL) crumbled dried savory

¼ lb (125 g) salt pork
3 cups (750 mL) peeled, diced potatoes

STOCK
Reserved chicken and rabbit bones
Cold water (see method)
1 small onion, coarsely chopped
1 stalk celery with leaves
1 tsp (5 mL) salt
½ tsp (2 mL) freshly ground black pepper
¼ tsp (1 mL) dried thyme leaves

PASTRY
2 cups (500 mL) all-purpose flour
1½ tsp (7 mL) baking powder
1 tsp (5 mL) salt
⅔ cup (150 mL) lard
½ cup (125 mL) milk
1 tsp (5 mL) white vinegar
1 egg, lightly beaten
Chili sauce or green tomato relish to serve

TO MAKE THE FILLING, cut the chicken and rabbit meat off the bones, discarding the chicken skin and reserving the chicken and rabbit bones for stock. Cut the meat into ¾-inch (2 cm) cubes. Cut the pork and beef into ¾-inch (2 cm) cubes. In a large bowl, mix together all the meats, the onions, celery, carrots, salt, pepper and savory. Cover and refrigerate overnight so that the flavours can mingle.

Meanwhile, make the stock. Place the chicken and rabbit bones in a large saucepan. Add at least 10 cups (2.5 L) cold water, so the bones are well covered, and bring to a boil. Skim off the foam. Add the onion, celery, salt, pepper and thyme.

Simmer, covered, over medium-low heat for 2 hours. Strain and refrigerate the stock until needed. Discard the bones and vegetables.

To make the pastry, mix the flour, baking powder and salt together in a large bowl. Using a pastry blender or two knives, cut in the lard until the mixture resembles coarse rolled oats. Add the milk and vinegar and mix in quickly to make a soft dough. Wrap in wax paper or plastic wrap and refrigerate until needed.

When ready to assemble the pie, preheat the oven to 400°F (200°C). Divide the pastry in half. On a lightly floured surface, roll out half the pastry to ⅓ inch (8 mm) thickness. Cut into 1-inch (2.5 cm) squares. Set squares aside.

Roll out the remaining pastry to fit the top of a 3- to 4-quart (3 to 4 L) flameproof casserole or Dutch oven (early versions of the recipe were baked in black cast-iron pots). Set aside.

Rinse the salt pork thoroughly under cold water to remove the excess salt. Drain and pat dry, then cut it into strips. In the casserole you're using for the pie, fry the pork strips over medium heat until crisp. Remove from the heat.

Top the pork with a layer of the meat mixture, then a layer of diced potatoes, then a layer of pastry squares, leaving space between the squares. Continue layering the meat, potatoes and pastry squares until everything is used up and the casserole is about three-quarters full. (There is some confusion in old recipes as to whether the six layers meant six layers of pastry or six layers in all. Either way is fine and depends on the shape of your casserole.)

Pour enough of the reserved stock into the casserole to come within 2 inches (5 cm) of the top. Reserve any remaining stock.

Dampen the edge of the casserole with water, then cover the casserole with the remaining pastry, sealing the pastry well to the edge of the casserole. Make a couple of slits in the centre of the pastry to allow the steam to escape, then brush the pastry with beaten egg.

Bake for 45 minutes, then reduce the temperature to 300°F (150°C) and bake for another 4 to 4½ hours or until the meat feels tender when pierced with a slender knife through one of the slits in the pastry. Check periodically during baking to make sure you can still see some liquid through the slits in the pastry. If the pie looks dry, pour in more stock using a funnel inserted in one of the slits. Serve hot with green tomato relish or chili sauce.

Cookies, Bars and Squares

I n the minds of Canada's German settlers, Christmas cookies were for children. The elaborately decorated treats were hung on boughs of evergreen, and later on Christmas trees, for children to enjoy and—of course—to eat.

The predominantly German custom of making cookies at Christmas caught on very quickly, so that despite the shortage of ingredients, most pioneer housewives made sugar cookies or gingerbread for the holidays. Today, most people make at least one or two types of cookies, while some make dozens.

This chapter features a wide variety of traditional Christmas recipes, some of which were brought to Canada from other lands, including the well-established Scottish shortbread. The first two recipes—Basler Leckerli and Christmas Fruit Cookies—require ripening time so be sure to make these well before the holidays. The remaining cookies in this chapter will keep for up to one week. Unless otherwise specified, cookies keep best in airtight containers, preferably in a cool dry place.

Basler Leckerli

Makes about 60 cookies

This chewy Swiss cookie should be made five weeks before
Christmas to allow ripening.

....

COOKIES
5¼ cups (1.3 L) all-purpose
   flour
2½ cups (625 mL) granulated
   sugar
2 tsp (10 mL) baking powder
1 tsp (5 mL) cinnamon
¼ tsp (1 mL) ground cloves

2 Tbsp (30 mL) honey
1 Tbsp (15 mL) water or
   brandy
1½ cups (375 mL) blanched
   chopped almonds
1½ cups (375 mL) diced
   mixed candied peel
4 eggs

ICING
⅔ cup (150 mL) icing sugar
2 tsp (10 mL) water
¼ tsp (1 mL) almond extract

TO MAKE THE COOKIES, grease a large baking sheet with a ½-inch (1 cm) rim. Preheat the oven to 350°F (180°C).

In a large bowl, sift together the flour, sugar, baking powder, cinnamon and cloves. Mix in the honey and water or brandy. Mix in the almonds and candied peel. Make a well in the middle of the mixture and in it place the eggs.

Using your hands, work the eggs into the flour mixture one at a time. Knead well in the bowl, then turn out onto a lightly floured work surface and continue to knead until the dough holds together and can be formed into a ball. (This step takes at least 5 minutes.)

Pat the dough out on the prepared baking sheet and, using a rolling pin, evenly cover the entire sheet with the dough. Bake for 10 to 15 minutes or until light golden.

Meanwhile, make the icing by stirring together the icing sugar, water and almond extract together in a medium bowl until smooth.

Spread the icing evenly over the warm dough. Cool on the baking sheet. Cut into small squares and store the cookies in an airtight container.

Christmas Fruit Cookies

Makes about 144 cookies

These German fruit cookies are a favourite in Mennonite homes. Make them well before Christmas to let their spicy flavour ripen.

....

½ cup (125 mL) lard, softened
½ cup (125 mL) butter, softened
1½ cups (375 mL) firmly packed brown sugar
2 eggs, beaten
¼ cup (60 mL) orange juice
1 tsp (5 mL) lemon extract
2½ cups (625 mL) all-purpose flour
1 tsp (5 mL) baking soda

1 tsp (5 mL) cinnamon
½ tsp (2 mL) ground cloves
½ tsp (2 mL) freshly grated nutmeg
½ tsp (2 mL) salt
2 cups (500 mL) chopped Thompson raisins
1⅓ cups (325 mL) chopped dates
1 cup (250 mL) finely chopped pecans

1 cup (250 mL) finely chopped walnuts
1 cup (250 mL) finely chopped hazelnuts
¾ cup (175 mL) diced candied citron
⅔ cup (150 mL) chopped candied cherries
½ cup (125 mL) chopped candied pineapple

GREASE LARGE baking sheets. Preheat the oven to 350°F (180°C).

In a large bowl, cream the lard and butter, add the sugar and beat until light and fluffy. Beat in the eggs, orange juice and lemon extract.

In a medium bowl, sift together the flour, baking soda, spices and salt.

In a food processor or by hand, chop all the fruit and nuts. (If using a food processor, do not process candied fruit too long, or it will become mushy.) Transfer the fruit and nuts to a separate bowl, add ½ cup (125 mL) of the dry ingredients and toss well.

Stir the rest of the dry ingredients into the creamed mixture, then add the floured fruit and nuts and mix well.

Drop slightly rounded tablespoonfuls (15 mL) of the dough, 2 inches (5 cm) apart, onto the prepared baking sheets. Bake for 12 to 15 minutes or until light brown.

Cool on racks then store the cookies in an airtight container for 3 to 4 weeks.

Forgotten Meringues

Makes about 60 meringues

One of the simplest treats to make, these meringues look quite
elegant on a plate of holiday dainties. "Forgotten" because they are.
You simply place them in the oven and don't need to think about
them until the next morning. Since they do not freeze well and are best
fresh, make them no more than a week before serving.

....

3 egg whites	1 cup (250 mL) powdered	Red and green food colouring
¼ tsp (1 mL) cream of tartar	fruit sugar	(optional)

LINE THREE LARGE baking sheets with foil.
Preheat the oven to 375°F (190°C).

In a medium bowl, beat the egg whites
until slightly foamy. Add the cream of
tartar and continue beating. When frothy,
gradually add the sugar, a little at a time,
beating until just stiff and glossy. (If you
beat the mixture too long after it is stiff, the
meringues may crumble.)

For a colourful selection of cookies,
divide the meringue mixture among three
bowls and carefully fold a few drops of
red food colouring into one portion and
a few drops of green food colouring into
the second portion, leaving the remaining
plain.

Drop teaspoonfuls (5 mL) of the
meringue onto the prepared baking sheets.
Place the baking sheets in the oven and
immediately turn off the heat. Do not open
the oven door for at least 12 hours. Store
the meringues in an airtight container.

Thimble Cookies

Makes about 36 cookies

Thumbprint cookies or Swedish tea rings are other names for
this old-fashioned cookie, which is found in many local cookbooks
from across the country.

....

½ cup (125 mL) butter, softened	1 egg, separated	¾ cup (175 mL) finely chopped walnuts
½ cup (125 mL) granulated sugar	1 tsp (5 mL) vanilla	Fruit jelly or jam
	1 cup (250 mL) all-purpose flour	

LIGHTLY GREASE LARGE baking sheets.
Preheat the oven to 350°F (180°C).

In a medium bowl, cream the butter,
add the sugar and beat until light and fluffy.

Add the egg yolk and beat well. Add the vanilla. Gradually stir in the flour until the dough is smooth.

Shape the dough into tiny balls. Dip each ball into the unbeaten egg white to coat completely, then roll in the chopped nuts. Using a floured thimble or the floured end of a wooden spoon handle, make a dent in the centre of each cookie. Place the cookies on the prepared baking sheets.

Bake for 5 minutes, then dent again with the thimble or the spoon handle and repair the sides of cookies if necessary. Bake for another 12 minutes or until set.

Cool on a rack, then fill each dent with a bit of jelly or jam. Store the cookies in an airtight container.

Old-Fashioned Chewy Ginger Cookies

Makes about 60 cookies

These cookies and Rolled Ginger Cookies (page 58) were brought to Canada by German settlers. They're delicious at Christmas and all year round, too.

....

1 cup (250 mL) granulated sugar
½ cup (125 mL) lard, softened
2 eggs
1 cup (250 mL) molasses
3½ cups (875 mL) all-purpose flour
1 Tbsp (15 mL) ground ginger
1¼ tsp (6 mL) baking soda
1 tsp (5 mL) ground cloves
½ tsp (2 mL) cinnamon
Additional granulated sugar

IN A LARGE BOWL, cream the sugar and lard together until light and fluffy. Beat in the eggs, one at a time, then beat in the molasses.

In a separate large bowl, sift together the flour, ginger, baking soda, cloves and cinnamon. Add the dry ingredients in three batches into the creamed mixture, mixing well after each addition. Knead the dough gently until smooth, then cover and refrigerate for 2 hours.

Lightly grease large baking sheets. Preheat the oven to 375°F (190°C).

Form the dough into 1¼-inch (3 cm) balls and roll them in granulated sugar. Place them on the prepared baking sheets and bake for 10 to 12 minutes, or until set. Cool on a rack and store the cookies in an airtight container.

Rolled Ginger Cookies

Makes about 180 cookies

The dough for these cookies can be rolled to make gingerbread men or houses. For gingerbread men, imbed raisins or currants in the dough before baking, or pipe on the decorative icing after the cookies have cooled.

···

COOKIES
1½ cups (375 mL) lightly packed brown sugar
1 cup (250 mL) butter
¾ cup (175 mL) molasses
1 Tbsp (15 mL) ground ginger
¼ tsp (1 mL) ground cloves

¼ cup (60 mL) hot water
1 tsp (5 mL) baking soda
5½ cups (1.37 L) all-purpose flour
1 egg, well beaten
½ tsp (2 mL) salt

DECORATIVE ICING
(optional)
2 cups (500 mL) icing sugar
2 small egg whites
1½ tsp (7 mL) white vinegar

TO MAKE THE COOKIES, combine the brown sugar, butter, molasses, ginger and cloves in a large saucepan. Stir over low heat until the sugar has dissolved and the butter melts. Bring to a boil, then remove from the heat and let cool.

In a small bowl, stir together the hot water and baking soda. Add to the molasses mixture, then stir in the flour, egg and salt. If the dough is too sticky, add a little more flour. Form the dough into a ball, wrap in wax paper or plastic wrap and chill for several hours or overnight.

Lightly grease large baking sheets. Preheat the oven to 350°F (180°C).

The dough will be very hard when it comes out of the refrigerator. Either let it return to room temperature before rolling, or cut slices from the chilled dough and roll them between two pieces of wax or parchment paper.

Roll out the dough to ¼-inch (6 mm) thickness and cut out the desired shapes either with cookie cutters or freehand.

Place on the prepared baking sheets and bake for 8 to 10 minutes or until lightly browned. Cool on racks.

To make the decorative icing, combine the sugar and egg whites in a large bowl and beat with an electric mixer at low speed until the mixture starts to hold its shape. Add the vinegar and beat at high speed until stiff and glossy. The icing hardens quickly, so do your piping promptly and apply decorative sugar or candies immediately. Store the cookies in an airtight container.

Old-Fashioned Sugar Cookies

Makes about 36 cookies

Through the years, most cookie jars have been graced by good old-fashioned sugar cookies. Although they are delicious all year round, these sugar cookies will be an attractive and tasty addition to your Christmas trays when garnished with bits of candied cherries, peel, nuts or coloured sugar, or decorated with an icing glaze.

....

1 cup (250 mL) butter, softened
½ cup (125 mL) lightly packed brown sugar
½ cup (125 mL) granulated sugar
1 egg
½ tsp (2 mL) vanilla

2 cups (500 mL) all-purpose flour
1 tsp (5 mL) baking soda
1 tsp (5 mL) cream of tartar
Coloured sugar, candied fruit or decorating candies for garnish

ICING GLAZE
(optional)
1 cup (250 mL) icing sugar
1½ Tbsp (22 mL) milk
Food colouring
Coloured candies or chopped candied cherries

IN A LARGE BOWL, cream the butter. Add the brown sugar and granulated sugar and beat until light and fluffy. Beat in the egg, then beat in the vanilla.

In a medium bowl, sift together the flour, baking soda and cream of tartar. Gradually add the dry ingredients to the creamed mixture, stirring only until thoroughly mixed. Divide the dough in half, wrap each half in wax paper or plastic wrap and chill for at least 3 hours.

Lightly grease large baking sheets. Preheat the oven to 375°F (190°C). Roll out one piece of dough to ¼-inch (6 mm) thickness or less. Cut the cookies into the desired shapes and, using a metal spatula, place on the prepared baking sheets, leaving 1½ inches (4 cm) between the cookies for

them to spread. Decorate with coloured sugar, candied fruit or decorating candies, as desired. (If you wish to decorate with icing glaze, do so after the cookies have been baked and cooled.)

Bake for 8 minutes or until lightly browned. Cool on racks.

To make the icing glaze, combine the icing sugar and milk in a small bowl. Stir until smooth. For a green or pink glaze, add a few drops of green or red food colouring and mix well. Spread the glaze on the cooled cookies. If you wish to garnish the glaze with coloured candies or bits of cherries, do so immediately before the icing becomes too hard. Store the cookies in an airtight container.

Chocolate Rum Balls

Makes about 30 rum balls

There are many recipes for these perennial Christmas favourites;
this one, containing almonds, is one of the best.

....

1 cup (250 mL) ground
   almonds
1 cup (250 mL) sifted icing
   sugar

1¼ tsp (6 mL) instant coffee
   powder
3 squares (3 oz/90 g)
   unsweetened chocolate

5 Tbsp (75 mL) dark rum
1 Tbsp (15 mL) milk
½ cup (125 mL) dark
   chocolate sprinkles

PLACE THE ALMONDS in a large bowl and sift in the icing sugar and instant coffee. In a food processor, process the chocolate until finely minced, or grate it using a cheese grater. Stir the chocolate into the almond and sugar mixture. Sprinkle 3 Tbsp (45 mL) of the rum and all of the milk over the dry ingredients, then mix until the mixture is evenly moistened and is a uniform dark brown. Cover and chill for 10 minutes.

Remove from the refrigerator, shape into a ball and knead several times. Form the mixture into ¾-inch (2 cm) balls.

Dip each ball into the remaining rum. Shake off the excess moisture and roll the balls in chocolate sprinkles to coat thickly. Place on parchment-paper-lined baking sheets to dry for 1 hour.

Place in an airtight container and refrigerate. Let the rum balls ripen for a few days before serving.

Date Dainties

Makes about 60 dainties

These tidbits don't require any cooking so they're fun and easy
for children to make—and eat!

....

1 cup (250 mL) smooth
   peanut butter
1½ Tbsp (22 mL) butter,
   softened
1 cup (250 mL) icing sugar

1 cup (250 mL) finely
   chopped pitted dates
¾ cup (175 mL) finely
   chopped walnuts

6 squares (6 oz/175 g)
   semi-sweet or bittersweet
   chocolate, chopped

IN A MEDIUM BOWL, cream the peanut butter and butter together. Add the icing sugar and beat until fluffy. Add the dates and walnuts and mix well.

Form small spoonfuls of the mixture into finger-shapes. (Dampening your hands will make shaping the dough easier.) Chill.

In the top half of a double boiler, in a heatproof bowl set over a saucepan of simmering water or in the microwave, melt the chocolate until smooth. Using a metal skewer, dip each finger in the melted chocolate. Place on a parchment-paper-lined baking sheet to set and cool. Store the cookies in an airtight container in the refrigerator.

Pecan Crescents

Makes about 72 cookies

I make Christmas cookies with my daughter-in-law Cherrie every year, and most of the recipes still come from the first edition of this book. My son Allen asks for his favourites to be baked, with these Pecan Crescents always on the list.

....

VANILLA SUGAR
¼ vanilla bean
1 cup (250 mL) icing sugar

COOKIES
1 cup (250 mL) butter, softened
½ cup (125 mL) icing sugar
2 tsp (10 mL) vanilla
2 cups (500 mL) all-purpose flour
½ tsp (2 mL) salt
2 cups (500 mL) finely chopped pecans

TO MAKE THE VANILLA SUGAR, cut the piece of vanilla bean into several pieces. Combine it with about 3 Tbsp (45 mL) of the icing sugar in a mini-chopper or a blender and blend at high speed until well integrated. (Alternatively, pound the ingredients together in a mortar and pestle.)

Add the vanilla mixture to the remaining icing sugar. Let the vanilla sugar sit for a day or two, so that the flavours can blend.

When you are ready to make the cookies, preheat the oven to 325°F (160°C).

In a large bowl, cream the butter, gradually add the ½ cup (125 mL) icing sugar and beat until light and fluffy. Add the vanilla.

In a medium bowl, sift together the flour and salt, and add to the creamed mixture. Fold in the pecans. Using 1 Tbsp (15 mL) of the dough for each cookie, shape into crescents. Place on ungreased baking sheets and bake for 25 minutes or until light golden brown. Gently sprinkle the vanilla sugar over the warm cookies to cover them completely. Cool completely on racks and store the cookies in an airtight container.

ALMOND OR HAZELNUT CRESCENTS
Follow the recipe for Pecan Crescents, substituting 2 cups (500 mL) finely chopped almonds or hazelnuts for the pecans.

Icebox Cookies

Makes about 72 cookies

Nowadays we would call these Refrigerator Cookies. The wrapped rolls of dough can be stored in the refrigerator for up to 10 days, or frozen for as long as a month.

....

½ cup (125 mL) butter, softened
1 cup (250 mL) granulated sugar

1 egg
2 Tbsp (30 mL) fresh lemon juice
2 cups (500 mL) all-purpose flour

½ tsp (2 mL) baking soda
½ tsp (2 mL) salt
Coloured sugar or decorating candies

IN A LARGE BOWL, cream the butter. Add the sugar and beat until fluffy. Add the egg and beat until very light. Stir in the lemon juice.

In a medium bowl, sift together the flour, baking soda and salt. Add the dry ingredients to the creamed mixture and mix well. Shape the dough into a roll about 2 inches (5 cm) in diameter, wrap in wax paper or plastic wrap and chill for about 1 hour.

Remove the roll of dough from the refrigerator and, without unwrapping it, roll it slightly on the counter so the cookies will be round when they're cut. Return the dough to the refrigerator and chill for several hours more or overnight.

When ready to bake the cookies, grease large baking sheets. Preheat the oven to 375°F (190°C).

With a sharp knife (an electric carving knife works well), cut the roll into slices about ⅛ inch (3 mm) thick. Leaving room for the cookies to spread, put them on the prepared baking sheets and sprinkle with coloured sugar or decorating candies. Bake for about 10 minutes, or until firm.

Remove from the oven and cool on racks. Store the cookies in an airtight container.

CHERRY-NUT COOKIES Follow the recipe for Icebox Cookies, adding 1 cup (250 mL) finely slivered almonds and ⅔ cup (150 mL) diced candied cherries to the dough. Omit the garnish.

LEMON-COCONUT COOKIES Follow the recipe for Icebox Cookies, adding ⅔ cup (150 mL) shredded coconut and 1 Tbsp (15 mL) grated lemon zest to the dough.

PEPPERMINT PINWHEELS Follow the recipe for Icebox Cookies, dividing the dough in half. To one half, add ½ tsp (2 mL) peppermint extract and a few drops red food colouring. Roll out each piece of dough separately between two sheets of wax or parchment paper to a 16- × 10-inch (40 cm × 25 cm) rectangle. Remove the top sheets of paper.

Invert the pink layer onto the plain layer and peel off the remaining paper. With the two rectangles of dough on top of each other, roll them up tightly, jelly-roll fashion, starting at a long side. Chill, slice and bake as for Icebox Cookies. These are pretty enough without any decoration.

CHOCOLATE-PEPPERMINT PINWHEELS
Melt and cool 2 squares (2 oz/60 g) of unsweetened chocolate. Follow the instructions for Peppermint Pinwheels, adding the melted chocolate and ½ tsp (2 mL) peppermint extract to one half of the dough and leaving the other half plain. Roll as for Peppermint Pinwheels. Chill, slice and bake as for Icebox Cookies.

Florentines

Makes about 24 cookies

Florentines make an elegant addition to a holiday cookie tray. This version features a particularly interesting combination of chocolate and orange peel.

⅔ cup (150 mL) finely chopped candied orange peel
⅓ cup (75 mL) blanched slivered almonds
¼ cup (60 mL) finely chopped golden sultana raisins

¼ cup (60 mL) all-purpose flour
½ cup (125 mL) whipping (35%) cream
¼ cup (60 mL) granulated sugar
3 Tbsp (45 mL) butter

1 tsp (5 mL) fresh lemon juice
1 cup (250 mL) semi-sweet chocolate chips
Tiny decorating candies (optional)

GREASE AND FLOUR large baking sheets. Preheat the oven to 350°F (180°C).

In a medium bowl, combine the peel, almonds and raisins. Add the flour and toss well.

In a medium saucepan, combine the cream, sugar and butter and bring to a boil. Remove from the heat and stir in the floured fruit and nuts and the lemon juice.

Drop tablespoonfuls (15 mL) of the mixture onto the prepared baking sheets, leaving room for the cookies to spread. Bake for about 10 minutes or until golden brown. Cool on the sheets for 2 minutes, then transfer the cookies to racks to cool completely.

In the top half of a double boiler, in a heatproof bowl set over a saucepan of simmering water or in the microwave, melt the chocolate until smooth. Turn the cookies upside down and brush melted chocolate onto the bottoms. Sprinkle tiny decorating candies on top of the chocolate, if desired. When the chocolate has set, store the cookies in an airtight container.

Lemon Cookies

Makes about 84 cookies

Lemon is one of my favourite flavours and here it gives
a simple sugar cookie a zesty hit.

....

1 cup (250 mL) butter,
  softened
4 oz (125 g) block cream
  cheese
1 cup (250 mL) granulated
  sugar

1 egg
1½ Tbsp (22 mL) grated
  lemon zest
¼ cup (60 mL) fresh lemon
  juice

3½ cups (875 mL) all-
  purpose flour
1 tsp (5 mL) baking powder
Coloured sugar (optional)

IN A LARGE BOWL, cream together the
butter and cream cheese. Gradually add the
sugar and beat until light and fluffy. Beat in
the egg. Stir in the zest and lemon juice.

In a medium bowl, sift together the
flour and baking powder. Gradually add
the dry ingredients to the creamed mixture
until well combined.

Shape the dough into a smooth ball,
wrap it in wax paper or plastic wrap and
chill for at least 3 hours or overnight.

When ready to bake the cookies, lightly
grease large baking sheets. Preheat the oven
to 375°F (190°C).

The dough will be quite hard when it
comes out of the refrigerator. Bring to room
temperature for a few minutes. Cut it into
quarters and roll out each quarter between
two sheets of wax or parchment paper to
⅛-inch (3 mm) thickness. Cut out cookies
with a cookie cutter and sprinkle each with
coloured sugar, if desired.

Place on the prepared baking sheets,
leaving room for the cookies to spread.
Bake for about 8 minutes, or until the
cookies start to become golden around the
edges. Cool on racks and store the cookies
in an airtight container.

Maple-Walnut Cookies

Makes about 132 cookies

Here's an updated version of a delicious cookie that was
popular in the days when maple sugar was the only sweetener
available to many pioneer families.

....

1 cup (250 mL) butter,
   softened
1 cup (250 mL) grated or
   granulated maple sugar
1 cup (250 mL) firmly packed
   brown sugar

2 eggs, well beaten
2 Tbsp (30 mL) water
1 tsp (5 mL) vanilla
3 cups (750 mL) all-purpose
   flour

2 tsp (10 mL) baking powder
1 cup (250 mL) finely
   chopped walnuts

IN A LARGE BOWL, cream the butter, add
the maple sugar and brown sugar and beat
until light and fluffy. Beat in the eggs. Stir
in the water and vanilla.

In a medium bowl, sift together the
flour and baking powder, and gradually add
to the creamed mixture. Stir in the nuts.
(The dough will be quite soft.) Wrap the
dough in wax paper or plastic wrap and
chill for at least 3 hours.

When ready to bake the cookies, lightly
grease large baking sheets. Preheat the oven
to 375°F (190°C).

The dough will be quite hard when it
comes out of the refrigerator. Cut the dough
into quarters and roll it out between two
sheets of wax or parchment paper to ⅛-inch
(3 mm) thickness. Cut into the desired
shapes with cookie cutters. Place, ¾ inch
(2 cm) apart, on the prepared baking sheets.
Bake for 10 minutes or until golden brown.
Cool on racks, then store the cookies in an
airtight container.

Scotch Bars

Makes 36 bars

This quick and delicious bar cookie, which originated in Scotland,
is easy enough for children to make.

···

BARS
½ cup (125 mL) butter,
softened
¼ cup (60 mL) granulated
sugar
¼ cup (60 mL) lightly packed
brown sugar

1 egg
½ cup (125 mL) all-purpose
flour
½ cup (125 mL) rolled oats
1 tsp (5 mL) vanilla

TOPPING
1 cup (250 mL) semi-sweet
chocolate chips
1 Tbsp (15 mL) butter
Chopped walnuts or coloured
shredded coconut

GREASE A 9-inch (2.5 L) square baking pan. Preheat the oven to 350°F (180°C).

To make the bars, cream the butter in a medium bowl. Add the granulated sugar and brown sugar and beat until light and fluffy. Beat in the egg. Stir in the flour, rolled oats and vanilla.

Scrape the dough into the prepared pan and bake for 20 to 25 minutes or until lightly browned. Remove from the oven and let cool in the pan for 10 minutes.

To make the topping, melt the chocolate chips and butter together in the top half of a double boiler, a heatproof bowl set over a saucepan of simmering water or in the microwave. Spread the chocolate evenly over the baked bars and sprinkle immediately with chopped walnuts or coloured coconut. Cool in the pan, then cut into bars.

Lemon Squares

Makes 48 squares

The lemon in the icing provides a refreshing topping
for these rich squares.

....

BASE
½ cup (125 mL) butter,
  softened
¼ cup (60 mL) firmly packed
  brown sugar
1 cup (250 mL) all-purpose
  flour

FILLING
1 cup (250 mL) firmly packed
  brown sugar

2 eggs, lightly beaten
1 tsp (5 mL) vanilla
1 cup (250 mL) finely
  chopped brazil nuts
1 cup (250 mL) chopped
  candied cherries
½ cup (125 mL) shredded
  coconut
1 Tbsp (15 mL) cornstarch
1 tsp (5 mL) baking powder
¼ tsp (1 mL) salt

ICING
3 Tbsp (45 mL) butter,
  softened
2 cups (500 mL) icing sugar
2 tsp (10 mL) grated lemon
  zest
2 Tbsp (30 mL) fresh lemon
  juice
Yellow food colouring
  (optional)

GREASE AN 11- × 7-inch (2 L) baking pan.
Preheat the oven to 350°F (180°C).

To make the base, cream the butter in
a medium bowl. Gradually add the brown
sugar and beat until light and fluffy. Stir
in the flour. (The mixture will be quite
crumbly.) Pat the mixture evenly into the
prepared pan.

Bake for 8 to 10 minutes or until light
golden. Cool in the pan for 20 minutes
before adding the filling. Leave the oven on.

To make the filling, lightly mix together
the sugar, eggs and vanilla. Add the nuts,
cherries, coconut, cornstarch, baking

powder and salt, and mix well. Pour the
filling over the base. Return to the oven and
bake for 35 to 40 minutes or until the filling
is set and light brown on top. Cool.

To make the icing, cream the butter in
a medium bowl. Gradually add the icing
sugar and cream it until light and fluffy.
Mix in the lemon zest and juice. Stir in a
few drops of food colouring, if desired, and
spread over the cooled filling. Cover tightly
and store for 1 day before cutting into small
squares. Store the squares in an airtight
container.

Apricot Bars

Makes 36 bars

Dried apricots are always good to have tucked away in your kitchen cupboard. They not only add flavour to both sweet and savoury dishes, but moisture and texture too.

....

BASE
½ cup (125 mL) butter, softened
¼ cup (60 mL) firmly packed brown sugar
1 cup (250 mL) all-purpose flour

TOPPING
¾ cup (175 mL) packed dried apricots
1 cup (250 mL) firmly packed brown sugar
2 eggs
⅓ cup (75 mL) all-purpose flour
½ tsp (2 mL) baking powder
¼ tsp (1 mL) salt
½ cup (125 mL) chopped pecans
1 tsp (5 mL) grated orange zest
½ tsp (2 mL) vanilla
Icing sugar

GREASE AN 8-inch (2 L) square baking pan. Preheat the oven to 350°F (180°C).

To make the base, cream the butter in a medium bowl. Gradually add the brown sugar and beat until light and fluffy. Stir in the flour. (The mixture will be quite crumbly.) Pat the mixture evenly into the prepared pan.

Bake for 8 to 10 minutes or until light golden. Cool in the pan for 20 minutes before adding the topping. Leave the oven on.

To make the topping, rinse the apricots and place them in a small saucepan with just enough water to cover them. Bring to a boil. Reduce the heat to medium-low and simmer, uncovered, for 15 minutes or until tender. Drain, cool and chop the apricots.

In a medium bowl, beat together the brown sugar and eggs. In a small bowl, sift together the flour, baking powder and salt.

Stir the dry ingredients into the brown sugar mixture. Stir in the cooked apricots, along with the pecans, orange zest and vanilla. Spread the topping over the baked layer. Return to the oven and bake for 30 minutes or until the top is golden. Do not over-bake.

Sprinkle the warm bars with icing sugar and cool in the pan before cutting into bars. Store the bars in an airtight container.

Christmas Fruit Squares

Makes 64 squares

These easy squares combine the pleasing flavours of orange and date and
are topped with an orange-rum icing.

....

SQUARES
½ cup (125 mL) butter,
  softened
1 cup (250 mL) granulated
  sugar
1 egg
2 Tbsp (30 mL) frozen orange
  juice concentrate
2 tsp (10 mL) grated orange
  zest
1 tsp (5 mL) vanilla

1 cup (250 mL) chopped
  pitted dates
½ cup (125 mL) chopped
  walnuts
½ cup (125 mL) diced mixed
  candied fruit
1¼ cups (300 mL) all-
  purpose flour, divided
½ tsp (2 mL) baking soda
¼ tsp (1 mL) salt

ICING
  (optional)
1 cup (250 mL) icing sugar
2 Tbsp (30 mL) butter,
  softened
1 Tbsp (15 mL) dark rum
1½ tsp (7 mL) orange juice
3 Tbsp (45 mL) diced mixed
  candied fruit
Granulated sugar (optional)

GREASE AND FLOUR a 9-inch (2.5 L) square
baking pan. Preheat the oven to 350°F
(180°C).

To make the squares, cream the butter
in a medium bowl. Add the sugar and beat
until light and fluffy. Beat in the egg. Stir
in the orange juice concentrate, orange zest
and vanilla.

In a separate medium bowl, toss the
dates, walnuts and candied fruit with ¼ cup
(60 mL) of the flour.

In a small bowl, sift the remaining flour
with the baking soda and salt. Add the dry
ingredients to the creamed mixture. Stir in
the floured fruit and nuts.

Spread the batter evenly in the prepared
pan. Bake for 30 minutes or until a skewer
inserted in the middle comes out clean.
Cool in the pan.

To make the icing, cream the icing
sugar and butter together in a medium
bowl. Blend in the rum and orange juice
and beat until smooth. Spread the icing
over the cooled mixture in the pan.
Decorate with candied fruit and cut into
small squares. (Alternatively, omit the icing,
cut into small squares and roll each square
in granulated sugar.) Store the squares in an
airtight container.

Light Rolled Shortbread

Makes about 60 cookies

Ever since the 19th century when Scottish settlers started
bringing recipes for this rich butter cookie to Canada, shortbread has
appeared on Canadian trays of holiday cookies and fancy cakes.

....

1 cup (250 mL) butter,
   softened
½ cup (125 mL) icing sugar

2 cups (500 mL) all-purpose
   flour

Decorating candies or
   chopped candied cherries

IN A MEDIUM BOWL, cream the butter thoroughly. Add the sugar and beat until light and fluffy. Add the flour a bit at a time and mix well. Form the dough into a ball, wrap it in plastic wrap and refrigerate overnight.

When ready to bake the shortbread, preheat the oven to 300°F (150°C).

Working with a small portion of the dough at a time, roll it out to ¼-inch (6 mm) thickness between two sheets of wax or parchment paper. Cut into the desired shapes with cookie cutters. Decorate with candies or pieces of cherry or simply prick three times with the tines of a fork.

Bake on ungreased baking sheets for 20 to 25 minutes or until firm. Do not let the cookies brown on top. Cool on racks and store the cookies in an airtight container.

Whipped Tender Shortbread

Makes about 48 cookies

This soft dough is just the right consistency for a cookie press,
if you have one, or you can drop it by small spoonfuls and use a cookie
print or a fork to make a design on top.

....

1 cup (250 mL) butter,
   softened
½ cup (125 mL) icing sugar

1½ cups (375 mL) all-purpose
   flour
½ cup (125 mL) cornstarch

Coloured sugar, decorating
   candies or chopped
   candied cherries

PREHEAT THE OVEN to 300°F (150°C).

Using an electric mixer, beat the butter in a medium bowl until very fluffy. Slowly add the icing sugar and continue to beat until light and fluffy.

In a separate medium bowl, sift together the flour and cornstarch. Add the dry ingredients very gradually to the creamed mixture, beating constantly.

Drop scant tablespoonfuls (15 mL) of

the dough onto ungreased baking sheets and press each cookie lightly with the floured tines of a fork. (Alternatively, put the dough through a cookie press.) Decorate the cookies with coloured sugar, candies or bits of cherry, if desired. Bake for 20 minutes or until firm. Do not let the cookies brown on top. Cool on racks and store the cookies in an airtight container.

Coconut Macaroons

Makes about 42 macaroons

These easy coconut macaroons have a lovely chewy texture.

....

3 egg whites
1 cup (250 mL) granulated
 sugar

2 cups (500 mL) shredded
 coconut

1½ tsp (7 mL) cornstarch
1 tsp (5 mL) vanilla

LIGHTLY GREASE large baking sheets. Preheat the oven to 325°F (160°C).

In the top half of a double boiler or in a heatproof bowl, beat the egg whites until stiff. Gradually beat in the sugar.

Put the double boiler or heatproof bowl over simmering water and cook over medium heat, beating constantly, for about 5 minutes or until a crust forms on the bottom and sides of the pan or bowl. Remove from the simmering water.

In a small bowl, mix together the coconut, cornstarch and vanilla. Add to the egg white mixture and blend well.

Drop teaspoonfuls (5 mL) of the mixture onto the prepared baking sheets.

Bake for 12 minutes or until light golden. Cool on racks and store the macaroons in an airtight container.

CHERRY-COCONUT MACAROONS
Follow the recipe for Coconut Macaroons, adding 1 cup (250 mL) chopped red and green candied cherries along with the coconut, cornstarch and vanilla.

CHOCOLATE MACAROONS Melt and cool 1 square (1 oz/30 g) semi-sweet chocolate. Follow the recipe for Coconut Macaroons, adding the melted chocolate along with the coconut, cornstarch and vanilla.

Holiday Breads and Festive Spreads

This chapter features a variety of holiday breads and rolls, from long-established Canadian favourites to the breads from other cultures that now enrich our Christmas traditions.

You'll notice that in some of the yeast-bread recipes, I give an approximate quantity of flour. There are many factors that affect the balance of liquid to dry ingredients—the temperature and humidity of your kitchen, for instance—and sometimes the flour will absorb more liquid than usual. There is one easy way to determine if enough flour has been added: when the dough is smooth and pliable and no longer sticky, there is no need to add more flour.

Yeast doughs need to rise in a warm, draft-free place. One easy way to achieve an even, gentle heat is to put the bowl of dough on a heating pad set to low heat.

All of the quick breads (the ones that don't contain yeast) in this chapter freeze well and can be sliced as needed without your having to thaw the whole loaf. Serve them buttered, or with the spreads that are included at the end of the chapter, for lunch, dinner or breakfast.

Fruited Pumpkin Loaf

Makes one 9- × 5-inch (23 × 12 cm) loaf

Serve this as an unusual Christmas cake or give it as a gift,
along with a jar of Pumpkin Marmalade (page 94).

....

½ cup (125 mL) butter,
softened
1 cup (250 mL) granulated
sugar
2 eggs

1 cup (250 mL) pumpkin
purée (not pumpkin-pie
filling)
½ tsp (2 mL) lemon extract
1½ cups (375 mL) diced
mixed candied fruit

2 cups (500 mL) all-purpose
flour, divided
2 tsp (10 mL) baking powder
¼ tsp (1 mL) salt

GREASE AND FLOUR a 9- × 5-inch (2 L) loaf
pan. Preheat the oven to 350°F (180°C).

In a large bowl, cream the butter. Add
the sugar and beat until light and fluffy.
Add the eggs, one at a time, beating well
after each addition. Stir in the pumpkin
purée and lemon extract.

In a medium bowl, toss the fruit in
2 Tbsp (30 mL) of the flour. In a separate
medium bowl, sift the remaining flour with
the baking powder and salt.

Add the dry ingredients to the pumpkin
mixture and blend quickly. Fold in the
prepared fruit.

Scrape the batter into the prepared pan
and bake for 1 hour and 20 minutes or until
a skewer inserted in the middle of the loaf
comes out clean.

Cool in the pan for 10 minutes. Remove
the loaf and cool completely on a rack. Wrap
and store for a day before serving. Serve cut
into slices and buttered.

Glazed Cranberry-Lemon Loaf

Makes one 9- × 5-inch (23 × 12 cm) loaf

This tangy holiday bread comes from British Columbia, where
a large percentage of Canada's cranberries are grown.

....

LOAF
¼ cup (60 mL) butter,
 softened
¾ cup (175 mL) granulated
 sugar
2 eggs
2 tsp (10 mL) grated lemon
 zest
1 cup (250 mL) chopped fresh
 or frozen cranberries*

½ cup (125 mL) chopped
 walnuts
½ cup (125 mL) diced candied
 mixed peel
2 cups (500 mL) all-purpose
 flour, divided
2½ tsp (12 mL) baking
 powder
1 tsp (5 mL) salt

¼ tsp (1 mL) cinnamon
¾ cup (175 mL) milk

GLAZE
1 Tbsp (15 mL) fresh lemon
 juice
2 Tbsp (30 mL) granulated
 sugar

GREASE AND FLOUR a 9- × 5-inch (2 L) loaf
pan. Preheat the oven to 350°F (180°C).

To make the loaf, cream the butter in
a large bowl. Add the sugar and beat until
light and fluffy. Beat in the eggs, one at a
time, beating well after each addition. Add
the lemon zest.

In a medium bowl, toss the cranberries,
walnuts and candied peel with ¼ cup
(60 mL) of the flour. In a separate medium
bowl, sift the remaining flour with the
baking powder, salt and cinnamon.

Add the dry ingredients alternately with
the milk to the creamed mixture, beginning
and ending with the dry ingredients. Stir
only enough to mix.

Stir in the floured cranberries, walnuts
and candied peel until all the ingredients
are well distributed. Do not over-mix.

Scrape the batter into the prepared
pan and bake for 1 hour and 10 minutes or
until a skewer inserted in the middle of the
loaf comes out clean. Cool in the pan for
5 minutes.

Meanwhile, to make the glaze, combine
the lemon juice and sugar in a small bowl.
Drizzle the glaze over the loaf. Let stand
for another 5 minutes in the pan. Remove
the loaf from the pan and cool completely
on a rack. Wrap and store for a day before
serving.

* If using frozen cranberries, there's no need
to thaw them first.

Glazed Tangerine Bread

Makes one 9- × 5-inch (23 × 12 cm) loaf

Although we don't grow citrus fruit in Canada, the holiday season brings
in the best from our southern neighbours so there's a good selection
of tangerines, clementines and all kinds of oranges available
at Christmastime. Here, tangerines lend an intense citrus flavour
to a moist quick bread that keeps well.

....

LOAF
5 to 6 medium-sized
  tangerines
⅛ tsp (0.5 mL) salt
¾ cup (175 mL) granulated
  sugar
⅓ cup (75 mL) water
⅓ cup (75 mL) butter, melted

1 egg, well beaten
2 cups (500 mL) all-purpose
  flour
2 tsp (10 mL) baking powder
1 tsp (5 mL) salt
⅔ cup (150 mL) chopped
  pitted dates

GLAZE
¼ cup (60 mL) icing sugar
2 Tbsp (30 mL) tangerine
  juice
1 Tbsp (15 mL) grated
  tangerine zest

FOR THE GLAZE, grate 1 Tbsp (15 mL) of zest from about 3 of the tangerines and set aside. Cut all the tangerines in half and squeeze out the juice. Measure ¾ cup (175 mL) juice for the loaf and 2 Tbsp (30 mL) for the glaze, and set aside.

Using a dessert spoon, scoop out and discard the flesh from four of the ungrated tangerine halves, discarding the remaining halves. Put the four scooped-out halves in a small saucepan and add enough cold water to cover them. Add the salt. Bring to a boil and cook, uncovered, for about 20 minutes or until the peel is tender. Drain, rinse with cold water and drain again. Scrape the inside of the peel to remove the bitter white pith. Chop the peel finely and set aside.

In the same saucepan, boil the sugar and water together for 5 minutes. Add the chopped peel and simmer, uncovered, over medium-high heat for 5 minutes. Remove the saucepan from the heat.

Grease and flour a 9- × 5-inch (2 L) loaf pan. Preheat the oven to 350°F (180°C).

In a large bowl, beat together the peel and syrup mixture, the reserved ¾ cup (175 mL) tangerine juice, the melted butter and egg.

In a medium bowl, sift together the flour, baking powder and salt. Add the dry ingredients to the tangerine mixture and blend quickly. Fold in the dates. Do not over-mix.

Scrape the batter into the prepared pan and bake for 1 hour and 10 minutes or until a skewer inserted in the middle of the loaf comes out clean. Cool in the pan for 5 minutes.

Meanwhile, make the glaze by combining the icing sugar, remaining 2 Tbsp (30 mL) tangerine juice and reserved grated tangerine zest in a small bowl. Drizzle the glaze over the loaf. Let stand for another 5 minutes in the pan. Remove the loaf from the pan and cool completely on a rack. Wrap and store for a day before serving.

Cherry Bread

Makes one 9- × 5-inch (23 × 12 cm) loaf

This easy bread uses ingredients you probably have on hand.
Always taste nuts before adding them to a recipe to check
that they're fresh. I usually keep nuts in the freezer; there's no need
to thaw them before using.

½ cup (125 mL) butter,
softened
1 cup (250 mL) granulated
sugar
2 eggs

2 cups (500 mL) all-purpose
flour
1 Tbsp (15 mL) baking powder
½ tsp (2 mL) salt
1 jar (6 oz/175 g) maraschino
cherries

Milk (see method)
½ cup (125 mL) chopped
walnuts

GREASE AND FLOUR a 9- × 5-inch (2 L) loaf
pan. Preheat the oven to 350°F (180°C).

In a large bowl, cream the butter. Add
the sugar and beat until light and fluffy.
Beat in the eggs, one at a time, beating well
after each addition.

In a medium bowl, sift together the
flour, baking powder and salt.

Drain all the syrup from the maraschino
cherries into a 1-cup (250 mL) measure. Fill
to the 1-cup (250 mL) mark with milk.

Cut the cherries in half. In a small bowl,
toss them with ¼ cup (60 mL) of the flour
mixture.

Add the rest of the dry ingredients to
the creamed mixture, alternating with the
cherry-milk mixture. Stir in the floured
cherries and walnuts, but do not over-mix.

Scrape the batter into the prepared pan
and bake for 1 hour and 10 minutes or until
a skewer inserted in the middle of the loaf
comes out clean.

Cool in the pan for 10 minutes, then
remove the loaf from the pan and cool
completely on a rack. Wrap and store for
a day before serving.

Candied Fruit Loaf

Makes one 9- × 5-inch (23 × 12 cm) loaf

I usually have a bit of mixed candied fruit left over after making
a fruitcake and this is an excellent way to enjoy it. The moist, colourful
quick bread is just right for afternoon tea.

....

¼ cup (60 mL) butter,
  softened
½ cup (125 mL) granulated
  sugar
1 egg
1 tsp (5 mL) vanilla
¾ cup (175 mL) diced mixed
  candied fruit

½ cup (125 mL) chopped
  walnuts
2 cups (500 mL) all-purpose
  flour, divided
2½ tsp (12 mL) baking
  powder
½ tsp (2 mL) salt

1 cup (250 mL) sour cream
½ tsp (2 mL) baking soda
¼ cup (60 mL) milk
2 tsp (10 mL) grated orange
  zest

GREASE AND FLOUR a 9- × 5-inch (2 L) loaf
pan. Preheat the oven to 350°F (180°C).

In a large bowl, cream the butter. Add
the sugar and beat until light and fluffy.
Beat in the egg and add the vanilla.

In a small bowl, toss the fruit and
nuts with ¼ cup (60 mL) of the flour. In
a medium bowl, sift the remaining flour
with the baking powder and salt. In a small
bowl, stir together the sour cream and
baking soda.

Add the dry ingredients, alternating
with the milk and the sour cream mixture
to the creamed mixture, beginning and
ending with the dry ingredients. Stir only
enough to mix. Stir in the floured fruit and
nuts and the orange zest.

Scrape the batter into the prepared
pan and bake for 1 hour or until a skewer
inserted in the middle of the loaf comes out
clean.

Cool in the pan for 10 minutes, then
remove the loaf from the pan and cool
completely on a rack. Wrap and store for a
day before serving.

Mincemeat Muffins

Makes 15 medium muffins

Sometimes bran muffins can be dry and flavourless but these, with mincemeat added to the mix, are moist and very delicious.

....

TOPPING
2 Tbsp (30 mL) firmly packed brown sugar
1 Tbsp (15 mL) all-purpose flour
½ tsp (2 mL) cinnamon
⅛ tsp (0.5 mL) ground cloves
2 tsp (10 mL) butter

MUFFINS
¼ cup (60 mL) granulated sugar
1 egg
1 cup (250 mL) bran
1 cup (250 mL) milk
¼ cup (175 mL) Mincemeat (page 41)

¼ cup (60 mL) vegetable oil
1 tsp (5 mL) vanilla
1 cup (250 mL) all-purpose flour
2 tsp (10 mL) baking powder
½ tsp (2 mL) salt
½ cup (125 mL) coarsely chopped walnuts

GREASE 15 MEDIUM muffin cups. Preheat the oven to 350°F (180°C).

To make the topping, combine the brown sugar, flour and spices in a small bowl. Cut in the butter until the mixture resembles rolled oats. Set aside.

To make the muffins, beat the sugar and egg together in a medium bowl. Stir in the bran, milk, mincemeat, oil and vanilla.

In a small bowl, sift together the flour, baking powder and salt. Add the dry ingredients to the mincemeat mixture. Stir in the walnuts. Do not over-mix.

Fill the prepared muffin cups three-quarters full and sprinkle with the prepared topping. Bake for 30 minutes or until a skewer inserted in the centre of a muffin comes out clean. Cool on a rack.

Snow Muffins

Makes 12 medium muffins

During the Christmas holidays, have some fun with your children and make these magic muffins. Have the other ingredients measured out and, just before you need it, collect the snow. Spoon it into the measuring cup—do not pack it in—then work quickly.

....

3 Tbsp (45 mL) butter
2 cups (500 mL) all-purpose
   flour
1 cup (250 mL) lightly packed
   brown sugar

1 Tbsp (15 mL) baking powder
1 tsp (5 mL) salt
1 cup (250 mL) milk
1½ cups (375 mL) clean white
   snow

¾ cup (175 mL) currants or
   sultanas

GREASE 12 MEDIUM muffin cups. Preheat the oven to 375°F (190°C).

In a small saucepan, melt the butter over low heat.

In a medium bowl, mix together the flour, brown sugar, baking powder and salt. Add the melted butter and the milk. Don't worry if the mixture is lumpy. Quickly mix in the snow and fruit, stirring only to blend.

Spoon into the prepared muffin cups and bake for 20 to 25 minutes or until a skewer inserted in the centre of a muffin comes out clean. Cool on a rack.

Cranberry-Oat Muffins

Makes 10 large muffins

I originally created these colourful, moist muffins for *Canadian Living*,
and they'd be a definite hit on any Christmas morning breakfast table.
If you wish, mix the dry ingredients with the oats and flour and prep the
sugar-cinnamon topping the night before, ready to put the muffin batter
together in the morning.

....

MUFFINS
¾ cup (175 mL) rolled oats (not instant)
1½ cups (375 mL) all-purpose flour
1 cup (250 mL) granulated sugar
2 tsp (10 mL) baking powder
½ tsp (2 mL) salt
½ cup (125 mL) cold butter
⅔ cup (150 mL) milk
1 egg
2 cups (500 mL) coarsely chopped fresh or frozen cranberries*

4 tsp (20 mL) grated lemon zest

TOPPING
4 tsp (20 mL) granulated sugar
1 tsp (5 mL) cinnamon

LINE 10 LARGE muffin cups with paper liners or grease them. Preheat the oven to 400°F (200°C).

To make the muffins, grind the rolled oats in a food processor, blender or mini-chopper until powdered, then transfer to a large bowl. Stir in the flour, sugar, baking powder and salt. Cut in the butter until the mixture is crumbly.

In a small bowl, whisk together the milk and egg, then pour over the dry ingredients. Sprinkle with the cranberries and lemon zest. Stir just until the dry ingredients are moistened. Spoon into the prepared muffin cups, filling them three-quarters full.

To make the topping, combine the sugar and cinnamon in a small bowl and sprinkle over the batter. Bake for 25 to 30 minutes or until the tops are firm to the touch. Cool on a rack.

* If using frozen cranberries, there's no need to thaw them first.

Stollen

Makes two 12- × 4-inch (30 cm × 10 cm) loaves

Stollen is a dense German fruit bread that takes its name from its shape—*stollen* means sticks or posts. The bread symbolizes the Christ Child in the crib.

....

1 cup (250 mL) blanched slivered almonds

1 cup (250 mL) diced mixed candied peel

½ cup (125 mL) halved candied cherries

½ cup (125 mL) golden sultana raisins

½ cup (125 mL) currants

⅓ cup (75 mL) finely chopped candied citron peel or ¼ cup (60 mL) finely diced angelica

5½ to 6 cups (1.37 to 1.5 L) all-purpose flour, divided

1¼ cups (300 mL) milk

½ cup plus 2 tsp (135 mL) granulated sugar, divided

½ cup (125 mL) butter

1 tsp (5 mL) salt

½ cup (125 mL) lukewarm water (110°F/43°C)

2 envelopes active dry yeast

2 eggs, slightly beaten

1 tsp (5 mL) grated lemon zest

½ tsp (2 mL) almond extract

⅓ cup (75 mL) butter, melted

¼ cup (60 mL) icing sugar

Additional icing sugar for sprinkling

IN A MEDIUM BOWL, toss the almonds, candied peel, candied cherries, raisins, currants, citron peel or angelica with ¼ cup (60 mL) of the flour. Set aside.

In a small saucepan, bring the milk just to simmering point then pour it into a large bowl. Add ½ cup (125 mL) of the sugar, the ½ cup (125 mL) butter and salt, and stir until the butter melts.

Meanwhile, dissolve the remaining sugar in the lukewarm water in a small bowl. Sprinkle in the dry yeast. Set aside for 10 minutes, then stir briskly and add to the milk mixture.

Stir in the eggs, lemon zest and almond extract.

Add 3 cups (750 mL) of the flour and beat until smooth. Gradually add enough of the remaining flour to make a stiff dough that leaves the sides of the bowl.

Turn the dough out onto a floured surface and knead for 10 minutes or until the dough is smooth and elastic. Press the floured nuts and fruit mixture into the dough a bit at a time. Do not handle the dough too much at this point or the bread will be discoloured.

Grease a large bowl with some of the melted butter and place the dough in it. Cover with greased wax or parchment paper and a towel and let rise in a warm place for 2 hours or until doubled in size.

Punch down the dough and divide it in half. Let the dough rest for 10 minutes, then roll each half into a 12- × 8-inch (30 × 20 cm) strip that's ½ inch (1 cm) thick. Brush each strip with 2 Tbsp (30 mL) of the melted butter and sprinkle each with icing sugar.

Bring one long side of each strip over to its centre and press the edge down. Fold in the other long side, overlapping the seam down the centre by about 1 inch (2.5 cm). Shape each loaf gently with your hands so that it mounds in the centre.

Grease two baking sheets, place a loaf on each and brush the loaves with the rest of the melted butter. Let the bread rise, covered, in a warm place for about 1 hour or until doubled in size. Meanwhile, preheat the oven to 375°F (190°C).

Bake the bread for 45 minutes or until golden brown and crusty. Transfer the loaves to racks to cool completely. Just before serving, sprinkle with additional icing sugar.

Stollen Glaze

Baked stollen is traditionally topped with a generous sprinkling of icing sugar but you can use this glaze if you prefer.

¾ cup (175 mL) icing sugar
1 Tbsp (15 mL) milk
¼ tsp (1 mL) almond extract

Diced candied peel or candied fruit (optional)

COMBINE ALL the ingredients in a small bowl. Beat until smooth, then spread on the hot baked stollen. If you wish, sprinkle a little diced candied peel or candied fruit on top.

Chelsea Buns

Makes 16 buns

Chelsea buns have been popular across Canada for many years. This very delicious version would be a treat for any holiday breakfast.

BUNS
1 cup (250 mL) milk
1 cup (250 mL) lukewarm water (110°F/43°C), divided
½ cup (125 mL) lard
⅓ cup plus 1 tsp (80 mL) granulated sugar, divided
2 tsp (10 mL) salt
1 envelope active dry yeast

5 cups (1.25 L) all-purpose flour
¾ cup (175 mL) red and green maraschino cherries
1 cup (250 mL) golden sultana raisins
½ cup (125 mL) pecan halves
½ cup (125 mL) butter, softened

¾ cup (175 mL) lightly packed brown sugar
1 Tbsp (15 mL) cinnamon

SYRUP
¾ cup (175 mL) lightly packed brown sugar
3 Tbsp (45 mL) butter
3 Tbsp (45 mL) hot water

TO MAKE THE BUNS, bring the milk just to simmering point in a small saucepan. Pour the milk into a large bowl and add ½ cup (125 mL) of the lukewarm water, the lard, ⅓ cup (75 mL) of the granulated sugar and the salt. Stir until the lard melts, then let cool to lukewarm.

In a small bowl, dissolve the remaining granulated sugar in the remaining lukewarm water. Sprinkle the yeast on top and let sit for 10 minutes, then stir briskly and add to the milk mixture.

Beat 2½ cups (625 mL) of the flour into the milk mixture, then gradually add enough of the remaining flour to make a soft dough.

Turn the dough out onto a floured surface and knead for 8 to 10 minutes or until the dough is smooth and elastic. Shape into a ball. Grease a clean large bowl and place the dough in it, rolling the ball to grease the entire surface. Cover with greased wax or parchment paper and a damp towel and let rise in a warm place for about 1½ hours or until doubled in size. Punch down the dough, knead two or three times, then let rest for 10 minutes.

Meanwhile, make the syrup by combining the brown sugar, butter and hot water in a small saucepan. Stir over medium heat until the butter melts, then boil for 2 minutes. Immediately pour the syrup into two greased 9-inch (2.5 L) square pans.

Drain the cherries thoroughly and cut them in half. Divide the cherries, raisins and pecans between the two pans, sprinkling them evenly over the bottoms.

Roll out the dough to a 14- × 9-inch (35 × 23 cm) rectangle. Spread the softened butter over the dough. Sprinkle with the brown sugar and cinnamon. Roll up from a long side into a tight roll. Cut crosswise into 16 even-sized pieces and place the pieces, cut-side down, in the prepared pans. Grease the tops, cover with greased wax or parchment paper and a damp towel and let rise in a warm place for about 45 minutes or until doubled in size. Meanwhile, preheat the oven to 375°F (190°C).

Bake the buns for 25 minutes or until golden brown. Place a sheet of wax or parchment paper under a large rack. As soon as the buns come out of the oven, turn the pans upside down on the rack. Allow the syrup to run over the buns and remove the pans. Cool on rack.

Beignets

(OLD-FASHIONED DOUGHNUTS)

Makes 24 doughnuts and 24 holes

Most early Canadian cookbooks and private recipe collections contained at least one doughnut, or "fried vices," recipe. Doughnuts keep well. Simply place them in a shallow baking pan and heat, uncovered, in a 350°F (180°C) oven for a few minutes.

....

2 Tbsp (30 mL) butter, softened
1½ cups (375 mL) granulated sugar
2 eggs, beaten
4 cups (1 L) all-purpose flour, divided

2 tsp (10 mL) salt
1 tsp (5 mL) baking soda
1 tsp (5 mL) cream of tartar
¾ tsp (4 mL) freshly grated nutmeg

½ tsp (2 mL) ground ginger
1 cup (250 mL) milk
Vegetable oil for deep-frying
Pinch of ground ginger
Icing sugar for sprinkling

IN A LARGE BOWL, cream the butter. Add the sugar and eggs and beat together until light and fluffy.

In a medium bowl, sift 3 cups (750 mL) of the flour with the salt, baking soda, cream of tartar and spices. Stir the dry ingredients into the creamed mixture, alternating with the milk.

Spread the remaining flour on your work surface. Turn the dough out onto the floured surface and gently knead it, incorporating only enough flour to prevent the dough from sticking (the less flour, the better). Wrap the dough in plastic wrap and refrigerate it for at least 3 hours.

Divide the chilled dough into quarters and roll out each piece on a lightly floured surface to a thickness of ⅓ inch (8 mm).

Cut with a doughnut cutter.

Meanwhile, in a large pot, heat the oil until it registers 375°F (190°C) on a candy thermometer. Add a pinch of ginger to the oil to prevent it from soaking into the doughnuts.

Using a slotted spoon, carefully place 3 or 4 doughnuts only in the hot oil at a time. Turning only once, fry the doughnuts for 3 to 5 minutes or until golden brown on both sides. Maintain the oil at a constant temperature.

Lift each doughnut carefully from the oil with the slotted spoon and drain thoroughly on paper towels. Cool and sprinkle generously with icing sugar. Don't forget to fry the holes—kids love them!

Butter Kringle

Makes 3 loaves

Kringle is a Danish Christmas bread traditionally made in the form
of a pretzel. The pretzel shape derived from a pagan calendar symbol
marking the winter solstice: a circle representing the sun's course
with a dot in the centre signifying the earth. This Icelandic version
from Manitoba is simply formed into long loaves, but in taste and texture
is identical to the Danish bread.

···

BREAD
1 cup (250 mL) milk
2½ Tbsp (37 mL) lard
2 Tbsp plus 1 tsp (35 mL)
   granulated sugar, divided
½ cup (125 mL) lukewarm
   water (110°F/43°C)
2 envelopes active dry yeast
2½ to 3 cups (625 to 750 mL)
   all-purpose flour
1 cup (250 mL) butter,
   softened

FILLING
¾ cup (175 mL) water
¾ cup (175 mL) chopped
   Thompson raisins
1 cup (250 mL) lightly packed
   brown sugar
¾ cup (175 mL) chopped
   pecans
½ tsp (2 mL) ground
   cardamom

TOPPING
1 slightly beaten egg
¼ cup (60 mL) granulated
   sugar
¼ cup (60 mL) blanched
   sliced almonds

TO MAKE THE BREAD, bring the milk just
to simmering point in a small saucepan,
then pour it into a large bowl. Add the lard
and 2 Tbsp (30 mL) of the sugar and stir
until the lard melts.

Meanwhile, in a small bowl, dissolve
the remaining sugar in the lukewarm water.
Sprinkle the yeast on top and let stand for
10 minutes. When the yeast bubbles up and
increases in volume, stir briskly and add to
the milk mixture.

Add 1½ cups (375 mL) of the flour
to the milk mixture and beat until very
smooth. Beat in enough of the remaining
flour to make a dough that leaves the sides
of the bowl. Remove the dough from the
bowl. Grease the bowl and return the
dough to it. Cover loosely with greased wax
or parchment paper and chill for 1 hour.
The dough will rise in the refrigerator.

Turn the dough out onto a floured
surface and roll into a thin 16- × 12-inch
(40 × 30 cm) rectangle. Spread one-quarter
of the softened butter over half of the
dough. Fold over the other half of the
dough and roll again, pounding the dough
with the rolling pin.

Place the dough on a greased baking
sheet, cover loosely with greased wax or
parchment paper and refrigerate for 1 hour.

Roll the dough out into a rectangle
again, spread with another quarter of the
softened butter and fold over the other half
of the dough. Roll again, pound and chill.
Repeat this process twice more.

During the last hour of chilling, make
the filling by bringing the water to a boil in
a small saucepan. Add the raisins and bring
to a boil again. Drain the raisins thoroughly
and dry on paper towels. In a small bowl,

mix the raisins with the brown sugar, pecans and cardamom.

Roll the dough out again to a thin 16- × 12-inch (40 × 30 cm) rectangle and cut lengthwise into three strips.

Place one-third of the raisin filling along the middle of each strip of dough. Fold the edges over to meet and seal all the edges well. Wrap loosely in greased wax or parchment paper and chill overnight.

When you're ready to bake the bread, preheat the oven to 425°F (220°C). Place the loaves seam-side down on greased baking sheets, leaving plenty of room for them to spread.

To make the topping, brush the loaves with the beaten egg. In a small bowl, mix together the granulated sugar and almonds, and sprinkle on the top of the loaves. Bake for 20 to 25 minutes or until browned on top. Serve warm.

The bread can be made well ahead of time and frozen. There's no need to thaw the loaves before heating. Simply wrap the frozen loaves in foil and reheat in a 375°F (190°C) oven for about 20 minutes.

Makivnyk

(POPPY SEED BREAD)

Makes 3 large loaves

At Svyata Vechera (Orthodox Christmas Eve dinner, on January 6),
Ukrainian Canadians enjoy a wide variety of breads and pastries.
Very often this sweet bread with its poppy seed filling is on the menu.
In some recipes, the loaves are bent into horseshoe shapes or placed in loaf
pans, but here they're baked freestyle as long loaves. Be sure to buy poppy
seeds from a reliable source since rancid seeds can ruin the bread.
Always store them in the freezer.

....

FILLING
2 cups (500 mL) poppy seeds
2 egg whites
½ cup (125 mL) granulated
 sugar
2 tsp (10 mL) grated lemon
 zest
½ tsp (2 mL) cinnamon

DOUGH
2 cups (500 mL) milk
½ cup plus 1 tsp (130 mL)
 granulated sugar, divided
½ cup (125 mL) butter
1 tsp (5 mL) salt
½ cup (125 mL) lukewarm
 water (110°F/43°C)
1 envelope active dry yeast
2 whole eggs
2 egg yolks

1½ tsp (7 mL) grated lemon
 zest
1 tsp (5 mL) vanilla
8½ cups (2.12 L) all-purpose
 flour (approx.)
1 egg white

GLAZE
1 egg, well beaten
1 Tbsp (15 mL) water

TO MAKE THE FILLING, cover the poppy
seeds with boiling water and soak for 1 hour.
Drain and dry thoroughly on paper towels.
Grind them in a mini-chopper or a blender.

In a medium bowl, beat the egg whites
until stiff peaks form. Fold in the sugar,
lemon zest and cinnamon, then fold in the
ground poppy seeds. Set aside.

To make the dough, bring the milk just
to simmering point in a small saucepan,
then pour it into a large bowl and cool to
lukewarm. Add ½ cup (125 mL) of the
granulated sugar, the butter and salt to the
warm milk. Stir until the sugar dissolves
and the butter melts.

In a small bowl, dissolve the remaining
sugar in the lukewarm water. Sprinkle the
yeast over the top and set aside for
10 minutes.

In a medium bowl, beat the whole eggs
and yolks well. Add the beaten eggs, lemon
zest and vanilla to the milk mixture. Stir
the yeast mixture briskly and add to the
milk mixture.

Add 4 cups (1 L) of the flour to the milk
mixture and beat thoroughly. Gradually add
enough of the remaining flour to make a
soft dough that leaves the sides of the bowl.
Turn out onto a floured surface and knead
for 8 to 10 minutes or until the dough is
smooth and elastic.

Grease a clean large bowl. Shape the
dough into a ball and place it in the bowl,
rolling the ball to grease the entire surface.
Cover with greased wax or parchment paper
and a damp towel and let rise in a warm
place for about 1½ hours or until doubled
in size.

When the dough has risen, beat the egg white in a small bowl until stiff peaks form. Punch down the dough and divide it into three even-sized pieces. Roll each into a rectangle about ¼-inch (6 mm) thick. Brush each rectangle with the stiffly beaten egg white (this keeps the filling from separating from the dough).

Spread one-third of the poppy seed filling over each rectangle. Starting from a long side, roll each rectangle up like a jelly roll and seal the edges by pinching together firmly. Place the rolls, seam-side down, on large greased baking sheets, leaving plenty of room for the dough to rise. Cover with greased wax or parchment paper and a damp towel and let rise for about 45 minutes or until doubled in size. Meanwhile, preheat the oven to 350°F (180°C).

To make the glaze, beat the egg and water together in a small bowl, then brush over the tops of the loaves. Bake for about 45 minutes or until they're golden brown and sound hollow when tapped on the bottoms. Cool on racks before cutting into slices.

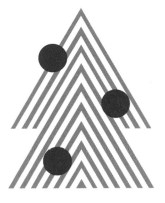

Bubble Bread

Makes 12 servings

Serve this unusual bread as a special Christmas morning breakfast with
fresh fruit, a creamy cheese (like Canadian brie) and coffee.

....

BREAD
1 cup (250 mL) milk
¼ cup plus 1 tsp (65 mL)
   granulated sugar, divided
¼ cup (60 mL) butter
1 tsp (5 mL) salt
¼ cup (60 mL) lukewarm
   water (110°F/43°C)

1 envelope active dry yeast
1 egg, slightly beaten
3½ to 4 cups (875 mL to 1 L)
   all-purpose flour
¼ cup (60 mL) red or green
   candied cherries
⅔ cup (150 mL) butter,
   melted

¾ cup (175 mL) chopped
   walnuts or pecans

GLAZE
½ cup (125 mL) corn syrup
3 Tbsp (45 mL) butter, melted
1 tsp (5 mL) vanilla

TO MAKE THE BREAD, bring the milk just to simmering point in a small saucepan. Pour the milk into a large bowl and add ¼ cup (60 mL) of the granulated sugar, the butter and salt. Stir until the sugar dissolves and the butter melts.

In a small bowl, dissolve the remaining sugar in the lukewarm water. Sprinkle the yeast over the top and let sit for 10 minutes, then stir briskly and add to the milk mixture. Stir in the egg.

Gradually add about 3½ cups (875 mL) of the flour to the milk mixture and beat well.

Sprinkle the remaining flour over your work surface and turn out the dough onto it. Knead the dough, incorporating only as much flour as necessary to keep the dough from sticking. Knead for 8 to 10 minutes or until smooth and elastic.

Grease a clean large bowl. Place the dough in it, rolling it to grease the entire surface. Cover with greased wax or parchment paper and a damp towel and let rise in a warm place for about 2 hours or until doubled in size.

Punch down the dough, turn out onto a lightly floured surface, knead a few times,
then let rest for 10 minutes.

Meanwhile, butter a 10-inch (4 L) tube pan. Arrange the cherries in the bottom. Pinch off bits of the dough and roll with your hands into 1-inch (2.5 cm) balls.

Arrange about one-third of the balls of dough, about ½ inch (1 cm) apart, in the prepared pan. Pour about one-third of the melted butter over the balls of dough and sprinkle with about one-third of the nuts. Repeat these layers twice until all the dough, butter and nuts are used. (If desired, more cherries may be placed between the layers of dough.) Cover with greased wax or parchment paper and a damp towel and let rise in a warm place for about 45 minutes or until doubled in size. Meanwhile, preheat the oven to 350°F (180°C).

Bake the bread for 35 to 40 minutes or until it sounds hollow when tapped.

To make the glaze, in a small bowl, mix together the corn syrup, melted butter and vanilla. Very carefully pour the glaze over the top of the hot bread in the pan. Let sit in the pan for 15 minutes. Place a sheet of wax or parchment paper under a rack. Invert the pan over the rack and remove the pan.

Serve hot by breaking off balls of bread into individual servings. To make ahead of time, wrap the cooled bread in foil and reheat before serving. The bread will keep well for a day or two and will freeze well.

Dinner Rolls

Makes 24 rolls

Since these delicate white rolls freeze very well, you can have them on hand for special holiday meals.

....

2 Tbsp plus ¼ cup (90 mL) granulated sugar, divided	2 envelopes active dry yeast	4 to 5 cups (1 to 1.25 L) all-purpose flour
½ cup (125 mL) lukewarm water (110°F/43°C)	1 cup (250 mL) buttermilk*	1 egg, beaten
	¼ cup (60 mL) lard, softened	½ tsp (2 mL) baking soda
	1 tsp (5 mL) salt	

DISSOLVE 2 Tbsp (30 mL) of the sugar in the water, sprinkle on the yeast and set aside for 10 minutes.

Pour the buttermilk into a large bowl and add the remaining sugar, the lard and salt. Stir in 1 cup (250 mL) of the flour.

Stir the yeast mixture briskly and add to the buttermilk mixture. Add the egg and baking soda, and mix well.

Mix in enough of the remaining flour to make a smooth dough. Turn the dough out onto a lightly floured surface and knead for 5 minutes or until smooth and elastic. Place the dough in a greased bowl, cover with greased wax or parchment paper and a towel and let rise in a warm place for about 1¾ hours or until the dough has doubled in size.

Punch down the dough. Shape into rolls and place them, 3 inches (8 cm) apart, on a large greased baking sheet. Grease the tops of the buns and let them rise for about 45 minutes or until doubled in size. Meanwhile, preheat the oven to 375°F (190°C).

Bake the rolls for 10 to 12 minutes or until they're golden brown and sound hollow when the bottoms are tapped. Cool on racks.

* If buttermilk is unavailable, stir 2 tsp (10 mL) fresh lemon juice or white vinegar into 1 cup (250 mL) milk and let stand for 10 minutes before using.

Herb Batter Bread

Makes one 9- × 5-inch (23 × 12 cm) loaf

Easy to make, this subtly flavoured herb bread goes very well
with cold turkey or chicken.

....

1 envelope active dry yeast
¼ cup (60 mL) lukewarm
   water (110°F/43°C)
¾ cup (175 mL) milk
3 cups (750 mL) all-purpose
   flour
1 egg

1 Tbsp (15 mL) granulated
   sugar
1 Tbsp (15 mL) vegetable oil
1 tsp (5 mL) salt
1 tsp (5 mL) dried marjoram
   leaves
¾ tsp (4 mL) dried thyme
   leaves

½ tsp (2 mL) dry mustard
½ tsp (2 mL) dried dillweed
Vegetable oil for brushing
Milk for brushing
Poppy seeds for topping

SPRINKLE THE YEAST over the lukewarm
water in a large bowl. Let stand to soften,
then stir briskly to dissolve the yeast.

In a small saucepan, bring the milk just
to simmering point, then remove from the
heat and cool to lukewarm.

Add 2 cups (500 mL) of the flour,
the milk, egg, sugar, oil, salt, marjoram,
thyme, dry mustard and dillweed to the
yeast mixture. Beat at high speed with an
electric mixer for 3 minutes (or 10 minutes
by hand). Stir in the remaining flour. Cover
with greased wax or parchment paper and a
damp towel and let rise in a warm place for
about 1 hour or until doubled in size.

Punch down the dough. Turn out onto
a lightly floured surface and knead about

20 times. Place the dough in a greased
9- × 5-inch (2 L) loaf pan, making sure the
dough fills the corners of the pan. Brush the
top of the dough with oil.

Cover with greased wax or parchment
paper and a damp towel and put in a warm
place to rise for about 45 minutes or until
doubled in size. Meanwhile, preheat the
oven to 375°F (190°C).

Brush the top of the loaf with milk and
sprinkle with poppy seeds. Bake for 40 to
50 minutes or until the loaf is golden brown
and sounds hollow when tapped on the top.
Remove immediately from the pan and cool
on a rack.

Orange Spread

Makes about ½ cup (125 mL)

Great with Candied Fruit Loaf (page 78), Glazed Cranberry-Lemon Loaf (page 75), Glazed Tangerine Bread (page 76), or with muffins or toast.

....

¼ cup (60 mL) butter, softened

2 Tbsp (30 mL) block cream cheese, softened

¼ cup (60 mL) icing sugar

2 Tbsp (30 mL) grated orange zest

IN A SMALL BOWL, cream the butter and cream cheese together well. Add the icing sugar and beat until light and fluffy. Blend in the orange zest.

Ginger-Nut Spread

Makes about ½ cup (125 mL)

Spread on Fruited Pumpkin Loaf (page 74), Snow Muffins (page 80), Mincemeat Muffins (page 79) or toast. Or fill the hollows in cored, cooked pear halves for use as garnish for meat and salad plates.

....

4 oz (125 g) block cream cheese, softened

2 Tbsp (30 mL) finely chopped candied ginger

2 Tbsp (30 mL) finely chopped pecans or walnuts

IN A SMALL BOWL, beat the cream cheese until light and fluffy. Blend in the ginger and nuts.

Cherry-Nut Spread

Makes about ½ cup (125 mL)

Use as a spread for Cherry Bread (page 77) or Mincemeat Muffins (page 79).

....

4 oz (125 g) block cream
cheese, softened

2 Tbsp (30 mL) well drained,
finely diced red and green
maraschino cherries

2 Tbsp (30 mL) finely
chopped walnuts

¼ tsp (1 mL) cherry extract

IN A SMALL BOWL, beat the cream cheese until light and fluffy. Blend the cherries into the cream cheese, along with the walnuts and cherry extract.

Pumpkin Marmalade

Makes ten 8 oz (250 mL) jars

This marmalade is a genuine treat and a convenient way to use pumpkins from the fall harvest long after the busy preserving season.

....

14 cups (3.5 L) ½-inch (1 cm)
cubes peeled, seeded
pumpkin (1 medium-to-
large pumpkin)

8 cups (2 L) granulated sugar

3 oranges

3 lemons

IN A LARGE non-reactive preserving kettle, mix the pumpkin and sugar together, stirring well to dissolve the sugar. Cover and let sit overnight.

Next morning, remove the pumpkin from the juice with a slotted spoon and set aside. Bring the pot of juice to a boil over high heat, then reduce the heat to medium-high and boil gently, uncovered, for 20 minutes.

Meanwhile, with a small sharp knife, remove the zest of the oranges and lemons, and set the zest aside. Remove all the bitter white pith underneath and discard it. Put the orange and lemon flesh and zest in a food processor and process until finely minced. (Alternatively, mince the flesh and zest very finely with a sharp knife. Don't use a blender for this; it will turn the fruit to mush.)

Add the pumpkin and minced citrus flesh and zest to the boiling juice. Gently boil everything together, uncovered, for 1½ to 2 hours, stirring very frequently, especially near the end of cooking time, until the pumpkin is translucent and the marmalade thickens and is a rich golden brown colour.

Remove the pot from the heat. Let the marmalade cool very slightly while you skim off any foam from the top with a metal spoon. (This will prevent the fruit from floating to the tops of the jars.)

Ladle into hot preserving jars, leaving ¼-inch (6 mm) headspace. Seal with discs that have been softened in hot water and rings. Boil in a boiling-water canner for 10 minutes. Remove the jars and let them cool on a rack. (The marmalade will set as it cools.)

Springridge Farm Christmas Marmalade

Makes nine 8 oz (250 mL) jars

Springridge Farm near Milton, Ontario, is a family fun farm that provides the kind of entertainment kids love, as well as fresh produce, baking and preserves. At Christmas, along with other holiday jams and gifts galore, their famous marmalade takes centre stage. Its creator, Jesse Lauzon, generously shared this easy recipe.

....

5 medium naval oranges (1½ lb/750 g)
3 cups (750 mL) water

7½ cups (1.87 L) granulated sugar

2 cups (500 mL) fresh or frozen cranberries, coarsely chopped*
1 tsp (5 mL) butter

WASH THE ORANGES and remove the stem end and any blemishes. Cut the oranges into pieces that will fit into the feed tube of a food processor. Fit the processor with the coarse shredding disc and shred the oranges. (Use a mini chopper, if you have one, for those stubborn bits at the end that won't go through the blade, or shred the bits very finely with a sharp knife. Don't use a blender for this; it will turn the oranges to mush.)

Combine the shredded oranges and the water in a large, deep, heavy-bottomed, non-reactive saucepan. Bring to a boil over high heat, then reduce the heat to low and simmer gently, stirring occasionally, for about 1 hour or until the orange shreds are very soft.

Stir in the sugar, cranberries and butter. Bring to a boil and cook, stirring gently with a long handled wooden spoon, for 12 minutes, being careful not to splash the hot marmalade.

Remove from the heat and stir for about 1 minute to cool slightly. Ladle into hot, clean preserving jars, leaving ¼-inch (6 mm) headspace. Seal with discs that have been softened in hot water and rings. Boil in a boiling-water canner for 10 minutes. Remove the jars and let them cool on a rack. (The marmalade will set as it cools.)

* If using frozen cranberries, there's no need to thaw them first.

Winter Apricot Conserve

Makes about nine 8 oz (250 mL) jars

This tart yet sweet spread makes a tasty Christmas gift.

....

1 lb (500 g) dried apricots
3½ cups (875 mL) cold water
1 jar (6 oz/175 g) red
   maraschino cherries
6 cups (1.5 L) granulated
   sugar

2½ cups (625 mL) undrained
   canned crushed pineapple
1 cup (250 mL) golden
   sultana raisins

4 tsp (20 mL) grated lemon
   zest
⅓ cup (75 mL) fresh lemon
   juice

CUT THE APRICOTS into small pieces with scissors, or chop them in a food processor. (Don't use a blender for this; it will turn the apricots to mush.) Place the apricots in a large heavy-bottomed saucepan, cover with the cold water and soak overnight.

Next morning, cook the apricots in the water in which they were soaked, uncovered, for about 15 minutes, or until tender.

Meanwhile, drain the maraschino cherries, reserving the juice. Cut the cherries into quarters with scissors and set aside.

Add the maraschino cherry juice, sugar, crushed pineapple with its juice, raisins, lemon zest and lemon juice to the apricots. Cook over medium heat, uncovered and stirring often, for about 1½ hours or until thick and clear. Add the maraschino cherries and cook for another 10 minutes.

Ladle into hot, clean preserving jars, leaving ¼-inch (6 mm) headspace. Seal with discs that have been softened in hot water and rings. Boil in a boiling-water canner for 10 minutes. Remove the jars and let them cool on a rack.

Potted Cheese

Makes about 3 cups (750 mL)

This sharp cheese spread should be prepared a week in advance so
that the flavours can mingle. It will keep for weeks in the refrigerator, but
allow it to come to room temperature for better spreading and flavour.

....

8 oz (250 g) old cheddar
  cheese
¾ tsp (4 mL) dry mustard

⅛ tsp (0.5 mL) onion salt
4 oz (125 g) block cream
  cheese, softened

¼ cup (60 mL) dry sherry
A few drops hot pepper sauce

SHRED THE CHEDDAR CHEESE finely,
preferably using a food processor fitted with
the fine shredding disc (this will make the
spread extra smooth and creamy), or use a
hand grater.

Add the dry mustard and onion salt, and
mix well. Blend in the cream cheese, then
add the dry sherry and hot pepper sauce.
Beat everything together until the mixture
is smooth and creamy.

Pack in a serving bowl, cover tightly and
store in the refrigerator. Serve with crackers
or melba toast.

Candies and Nibbles

s soon as sugar became available in the 19th century, people began making candy as an extremely special treat for holiday eating and for decorating the Christmas tree. Today, candy is an indispensable part of the Christmas tradition.

Although candy-making demands accuracy and care, it isn't difficult. Even if you have never made candy before, by following the recipes closely and using a candy thermometer (see below) you will soon have dozens of homemade treats for your family and friends to enjoy.

Here are some tips to help make preparing candy easy and enjoyable.

USE THE RIGHT SAUCEPAN

Sugar burns easily and more than doubles in size when it boils, so always use a large, heavy-bottomed saucepan for making candy. Buttering or oiling the saucepan before adding the ingredients will help keep the mixture from sticking.

A THERMOMETER'S A MUST

Forget the fact that your grandmother made countless batches of perfect fudge without the aid of a candy thermometer. Invest in one and you'll find making candy is much easier. Sugar passes through a number of definite stages when it is heated and ensuring it's cooked long enough and gets to the right temperature are important factors in the success of the finished product.

TO STIR OR NOT TO STIR

It is important to follow the instructions for stirring the syrup for a candy. Stirring at the wrong stage will affect the texture of the finished product.

Creamy Chocolate Fudge

Makes 36 pieces

No one can resist chocolate, especially when it appears in melt-in-your-mouth creamy fudge. To cool a fudge mixture quickly so you can beat it, pour the hot mixture into a bowl and set the bowl in the sink (or in a bigger bowl) filled with about 2 inches (5 cm) of cold water.

....

2 squares (2 oz/60 g) unsweetened chocolate
2 cups (500 mL) granulated sugar

⅔ cup (150 mL) evaporated milk or half-and-half (10%) cream

2 Tbsp (30 mL) corn syrup
3 Tbsp (45 mL) butter
1 tsp (5 mL) vanilla

GREASE AN 8-inch (2 L) square baking pan with butter. Grease the inside of a medium heavy-bottomed saucepan with butter.

Grate the chocolate into the saucepan and add the sugar, evaporated milk and corn syrup. Stir over low heat until the chocolate melts and sugar has dissolved. Increase the heat to medium and bring to a boil, stirring constantly. Boil, without stirring, until the mixture registers 240°F (115°C) on a candy thermometer and forms a soft ball when a little is dropped into a bowl of cold water.

Remove the saucepan from the heat and add the butter but do not stir. Cool to lukewarm (110°F/43°C on a candy thermometer) without stirring.

Add the vanilla, then beat until the fudge loses its gloss and becomes thick enough to hold its shape. (This will take 8 to 10 minutes if you use a heavy-duty electric mixer and longer by hand.) Immediately pat the fudge into the prepared pan. Cool, then cut into squares.

Maple-Cream Fudge

Makes 36 pieces

My mother, Josephine Varty, always made this absolutely delicious,
creamy fudge (without a candy thermometer!) and always called
it Maple-Cream Fudge despite the fact there was no maple syrup
in it. I've checked in some older cookbooks and they also
give the candy the same name. I imagine it came from the
brown sugar lending a certain "mapleness."

....

4 cups (1 L) lightly packed
  brown sugar
1 cup (250 mL) evaporated
  milk or half-and-half (10%)
  cream

2 Tbsp (30 mL) all-purpose
  flour
2 tsp (10 mL) baking powder

⅛ tsp (0.5 mL) salt
¼ cup (60 mL) butter
1 tsp (5 mL) vanilla

GREASE AN 8-inch (2 L) square baking pan
with butter. Grease the inside of a large
heavy-bottomed saucepan with butter.

In the saucepan, combine the brown
sugar, evaporated milk, flour, baking
powder and salt. Stir over low heat until
the sugar has dissolved. Increase the heat
to medium and bring to a boil, stirring
constantly. Boil, without stirring, until the
mixture registers 240°F (115°C) on a candy
thermometer and forms a soft ball when a
little is dropped into a bowl of cold water.

Remove the saucepan from the heat
and add the butter but do not stir. Cool
to lukewarm (110°F/43°C on a candy
thermometer) without stirring.

Add the vanilla, then beat until the
fudge loses its gloss and becomes thick
enough to hold its shape. (This will

take 8 to 10 minutes if you use a heavy-
duty electric mixer and longer by hand.)
Immediately scrape the fudge into the
prepared pan and smooth the top. Let cool
until firm, then cut into squares. If the
fudge becomes too stiff to scrape into the
pan, knead it until it softens then press the
fudge into the pan. (Alternatively, shape the
fudge into a 1- to 2-inch/2.5 to 5 cm thick
log, then cut into slices.)

If the fudge doesn't set, scrape it back
into the saucepan and stir in ¼ cup (60 mL)
milk. Boil again, without stirring, until the
mixture registers 240°F (115°C) on a candy
thermometer and forms a soft ball when a
little is dropped into a bowl of cold water.
Cool as above, then beat the fudge again
until it reaches the right consistency.

White Christmas Fudge

Makes 36 pieces

This delicious fudge—also called Divinity Fudge, possibly because it tastes divine—will keep soft for weeks if stored in an airtight container in a cool place.

....

3 cups (750 mL) granulated sugar
1½ cups (375 mL) half-and-half (10%) cream
1 cup (250 mL) corn syrup

1½ tsp (7 mL) vanilla
1 cup (250 mL) diced red and green candied cherries
1 cup (250 mL) diced candied pineapple

¾ cup (175 mL) pecan halves
¾ cup (175 mL) chopped walnuts

GREASE AN 8-inch (2 L) square baking pan with butter. Grease the inside of a large heavy-bottomed saucepan with butter.

In the saucepan, combine the sugar, cream and corn syrup. Cook over low heat, stirring until the sugar has dissolved. Increase the heat to medium and bring to a boil, stirring constantly. Boil, without stirring, until the mixture registers 240°F (115°C) on a candy thermometer and forms a soft ball when a little is dropped into a bowl of cold water.

Remove the saucepan from the heat. Beat immediately until it begins to lose its gloss and becomes thick enough to hold its shape. (This will take 8 to 10 minutes if you use a heavy-duty electric mixer and longer by hand.)

Drop a spoonful of the mixture onto parchment paper. If it stays in a mound, it has been beaten long enough. If it flattens out, beat for another 30 seconds and check again. If still not set, transfer it to a bowl and place over boiling water and continue beating. If the mixture becomes too stiff, beat in a few drops of hot water.

Add the vanilla and slowly stir in the fruit and nuts. Pat into the prepared pan. Chill, then cut into squares.

Pulled Toffee

Makes about 2 lb (1 kg) toffee

Why not introduce children to the fun of making this old-fashioned
Canadian candy? Once the toffee has cooled slightly,
they can help you pull and stretch it.

....

½ cup (125 mL) water
2 cups (500 mL) lightly
   packed brown sugar

2 cups (500 mL) molasses
2 Tbsp (30 mL) vinegar

1 Tbsp (15 mL) butter
½ tsp (2 mL) baking soda

GREASE A large baking sheet with butter.

In a large heavy-bottomed saucepan, bring the water to a boil. Stir in the brown sugar, molasses, vinegar and butter. Boil, without stirring, until the mixture registers 260°F (127°C) on a candy thermometer and forms a hard ball when a little is dropped into a bowl of cold water. Add the baking soda and mix well. Remove the saucepan from the heat.

Pour the toffee onto the prepared baking sheet. With a metal spatula, fold the edges of the toffee toward the centre. Repeat several times until the mixture is cool enough to be pulled by hand and only a dent remains when pressed with a finger (this takes a few minutes).

Thoroughly grease your hands with butter, then pull and stretch the toffee over and over again. (It's fun to let children help you with this part.) Work quickly because the toffee hardens very fast. The toffee will become lighter in colour as it hardens.

When the toffee is too hard to pull, place it on a baking sheet and roll out into a thin slab. Grease the blades of a pair of scissors or a heavy knife with butter, then cut the slab of toffee into 1½-inch (4 cm) pieces. Wrap each piece of toffee in a small square of wax or parchment paper.

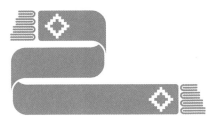

Filled Dates

Makes about 60 dates

Choose large, fresh-looking dates for these easy treats that keep well
for up to two weeks if refrigerated in an airtight container.

½ cup (125 mL) Traditional
Almond Paste (page 20)
1 Tbsp (15 mL) dark rum
1 cup (250 mL) icing sugar
3 Tbsp (45 mL) finely
chopped walnuts

2 Tbsp (30 mL) finely
chopped dried apricots
1 tsp (5 mL) finely chopped
crystallized ginger
2 lb (1 kg) loosely packed
pitted dates (approx.)

Granulated sugar or melted
unsweetened chocolate for
coating

IN A MEDIUM BOWL, combine the almond
paste and rum, kneading with your hands
to moisten the paste. Gradually blend in the
icing sugar. Stir in the walnuts, apricots and
ginger.

Shape teaspoonfuls of the paste into
small ovals and use to fill the hollow in

the dates left by the pit. Roll the dates in
granulated sugar or dip in melted chocolate.
If using chocolate, place the dates on a
parchment-paper-lined baking sheet to set
before storing in an airtight container.

Candied Citrus Peel

Makes about 2 cups (500 mL)

Candied peel is an elegant accompaniment to after-dinner coffee, and a
flavourful change from commercial peel in cakes and breads. If you prefer,
use four oranges in place of the two oranges and one grapefruit.

2 large oranges
1 grapefruit

1¾ cups (425 mL) granulated
sugar
¾ cup (175 mL) water

Additional granulated sugar
for coating

WITH A VERY FINE grater, lightly smooth
the outer surface of the citrus fruit but do
not remove much of the colour. Score the
fruit into quarters with a sharp knife, then
remove the peel, reserving the fruit for
eating or for use in another recipe. Place the

peel in a saucepan, add enough cold water
to cover it and soak for 1 hour.

Drain the peel, cover it again with cold
water and bring slowly to a boil. Drain
again and repeat the process. Cover again
with cold water, bring slowly to a boil, then

simmer, covered, for 20 minutes or until the rind is very tender. Drain.

When the peel is cool enough to handle, scrape the inside of the rind to remove any of the bitter white pith. Using scissors, cut the rind into ¼-inch (6 mm) strips.

In a medium saucepan, combine the sugar and ¾ cup (175 mL) water and bring to a boil. Add the peel and cook gently, uncovered, for 20 minutes or until the peel is translucent and has absorbed most of the syrup. Remove the saucepan from the heat and cool the peel in the syrup.

Reheat gently just enough that the peel can be lifted out of the syrup. Separate the strips and place on a parchment-paper-lined baking sheet. Put a small amount of granulated sugar in a small paper bag and shake the peel in it, a few strips at a time. Put the peel back on the baking sheet and let dry at room temperature for at least 1 hour.

The candied peel will keep indefinitely if stored in an airtight container and will actually improve in taste after 2 to 3 weeks.

CHOCOLATE-ORANGE PEEL For a delicious variation, dip the candied citrus peel in melted semi-sweet chocolate instead of shaking it in granulated sugar.

Popcorn Balls

Makes ten 2-inch (5 cm) balls

Long strings of popcorn adorned the branches of Victorian Christmas trees. We can still enjoy this traditional decoration on the tree, but pop some extra corn for these candy popcorn balls that make fun treats.

....

8 cups (2 L) freshly popped popcorn	½ cup (125 mL) corn syrup	¼ tsp (1 mL) salt
	¼ cup (60 mL) white vinegar	1 tsp (5 mL) vanilla
1½ cups (375 mL) firmly packed brown sugar	2 Tbsp (30 mL) butter	
	2 Tbsp (30 mL) water	

PUT THE POPCORN in a large heatproof bowl.

In a large heavy-bottomed saucepan, combine the brown sugar, corn syrup, vinegar, butter, water and salt. Stir over medium heat until the mixture comes to a boil. Cook, without stirring, until the mixture registers 260°F (125°C) on a candy thermometer and forms a hard ball when a little is dropped into a bowl of cold water.

Remove the saucepan from the heat and add the vanilla. Immediately pour the sugar mixture over the popcorn and mix quickly, making sure to coat all of the popped kernels. Wet your hands with cold water and press ¼ to ⅓ cup (60 to 75 mL) of the coated popcorn into a firm 2-inch (5 cm) ball. Place on a parchment-paper-lined baking sheet to cool. Repeat with the remaining coated popcorn.

RICE-NUT BALLS Follow the recipe for Popcorn Balls, substituting 7 cups (1.75 L) puffed rice cereal and ¾ cup (175 mL) coarsely chopped peanuts for the popcorn.

Homemade Filled Chocolates

Makes about 144 chocolates

As a child growing up on our farm, I remember helping to make
these with our neighbours. While the men shredded and
packed the cabbage for the winter's sauerkraut, the women would
make chocolates for Christmas gifts.

The uncooked fondant that fills these chocolates is so simple to make
that your children can help you create them for Christmas gifts. If you
have any melted chocolate left over after coating the fondant centres, try
dipping candied peel, brandied cherries, bite-sized pieces of crystallized
ginger or whole nuts into it to add variety to your chocolate box.

....

FONDANT
½ cup (125 mL) butter,
   softened
11 cups (2.75 L) icing sugar
1⅓ cups (325 mL) sweetened
   condensed milk

3 Tbsp (45 mL) corn syrup
Food colouring

FLAVOURINGS AND
   FILLINGS
See list on facing page

COATING
8 squares (8 oz/250 g)
   unsweetened chocolate,
   chopped

TO MAKE THE FONDANT, cream the
butter thoroughly in a very large bowl.
Gradually mix in the icing sugar. Stir in
the condensed milk and corn syrup and
mix until well combined. Turn the fondant
out onto a work surface lightly dusted with
icing sugar and knead until smooth.

Divide the fondant into as many small
bowls as you have flavourings and fillings
(see list on facing page). Knead in food
colouring to tint the fondant as desired.

Knead about ¼ tsp (1 mL) (or to taste)
of your chosen flavouring into each bowl of
fondant. Make fondant centres by rolling
about 1 tsp (5 mL) of fondant around each
filling, using a bit more fondant for those
without fruit or nuts.

Place the finished fondant centres on a
parchment-paper-lined baking sheet and let
dry at room temperature for a few minutes
before you coat them, or store them in an

airtight container overnight and coat them
the next day.

To make the coating, in the top half of
a double boiler or in a heatproof bowl set
over a saucepan of simmering water, melt
the chocolate until smooth. Remove the
double boiler or saucepan from the heat but
keep the chocolate over the hot water while
dipping the fondant centres.

Line a chilled baking sheet with wax
or parchment paper. Using a small metal
skewer or a special scoop for dipping
(available in kitchen shops), spear the
fondant centres one at a time and quickly
dip into the melted chocolate, rolling to
cover the fondant completely. Let them
drip well to remove the excess chocolate,
then place on the baking sheet to harden.
Store in an airtight container in a cool, dark
place. Serve the chocolates in paper candy
cases.

Almond extract and candied
   cherries
Lemon extract and candied
   lemon peel
Maple flavouring and walnut
   halves
Melted chocolate and instant
   coffee powder

Melted chocolate and
   peppermint extract
Orange extract and candied
   orange peel
Orange extract and pecan
   halves
Peppermint extract
Rum and peanuts

Vanilla and candied ginger
Vanilla and well-drained
   maraschino cherries
   soaked in brandy and well
   drained again
Vanilla and whole hazelnuts,
   brazil nuts or almonds

Spiced Nuts

Makes about 4 cups (1 L)

It's always good to have something interesting on hand to serve
with a holiday drink. These spicy nuts go well with a mulled cider
or a glass of sherry.

2 cups (500 mL) walnut
   halves
1 cup (250 mL) whole
   blanched almonds
½ cup (125 mL) pecan halves

2 egg whites
Pinch of salt
1 cup (250 mL) granulated
   sugar
1 tsp (5 mL) cinnamon

¼ tsp (1 mL) freshly grated
   nutmeg
¼ tsp (1 mL) ground allspice
½ cup (125 mL) butter
½ tsp (2 mL) salt

PREHEAT THE OVEN to 300°F (150°C).
Spread out all of the nuts in a single layer
on a large rimmed baking sheet and toast in
the oven for about 10 minutes or until light
brown. Leave the oven on.

   Meanwhile, in a large bowl, beat the
egg whites and salt until soft peaks form.
Gradually add the sugar and beat until stiff.

   Fold in the spices until well combined,
then fold in the toasted nuts.

   Put the butter on the baking sheet you
used for the nuts and heat in the oven for
2 to 3 minutes or until the butter melts.
Spread the nut mixture out on the baking
sheet and sprinkle with salt. Bake for about
30 minutes, stirring often, until the nuts are
brown and no butter remains on the baking
sheet. Tip the nut mixture out onto a large
sheet of foil and cool.

Glazed Almonds

Makes about 1½ cups (375 mL)

You can also use unblanched almonds and sea salt (instead of table salt)
for these delicious nibbles.

⅓ cup (75 mL) granulated
   sugar
2 Tbsp (30 mL) butter

1 Tbsp (15 mL) corn syrup
1 cup (250 mL) whole
   blanched almonds

½ tsp (2 mL) vanilla
¼ tsp (1 mL) salt

LINE A LARGE baking sheet with foil.
   In a heavy skillet, combine the sugar, butter and corn syrup. Bring to a boil over medium heat, stirring constantly. Add the almonds and cook, stirring almost constantly, for about 10 minutes or until the nuts are golden brown. Stir in the vanilla.

Spread the nut mixture in a single layer on the baking sheet. Sprinkle with salt. Cool, then break into clusters of 2 or 3 nuts.

GLAZED MIXED NUTS

Follow the recipe for Glazed Almonds, substituting pecans, walnuts and/or peanuts for the almonds.

Peanut Brittle

Makes about 2 lb (1 kg)

This sturdy and long-keeping favourite candy is a great choice for gifts.

2 cups (500 mL) granulated
   sugar
1 cup (250 mL) corn syrup

1 cup (250 mL) water
2 cups (500 mL) salted or
   unsalted roasted peanuts

2 Tbsp (30 mL) butter
¾ tsp (4 mL) baking soda

LIGHTLY OIL two large baking sheets. Grease the inside of a large heavy-bottomed saucepan with oil.
   In the saucepan, combine the sugar, corn syrup and water. Stirring constantly, heat until the sugar has dissolved. Boil over medium-high heat, stirring often, until the mixture registers 240°F (115°C) on a candy thermometer and forms a soft ball when a little is dropped into a bowl of cold water.

Continue boiling over medium-high heat, without stirring, until the mixture registers 280°F (137°C) and separates into hard yet pliable threads when a little is dropped into a bowl of cold water.
   Stir in the peanuts and butter. Continue boiling over medium-high heat, stirring occasionally, until the mixture registers 300°F (149°C) and separates into hard, brittle threads when a little is dropped into

a bowl of cold water. Remove the saucepan from the heat and immediately stir in the baking soda.

Quickly pour the candy onto the prepared baking sheets. As the candy cools, stretch it out by lifting and pulling the edges. Loosen the peanut brittle from the sheets as soon as it hardens and turn the candy over. Cool, then break it into chunks.

COCONUT-ORANGE BRITTLE Follow the Peanut Brittle recipe, substituting 1½ cups (375 mL) shredded coconut and 1½ tsp (7 mL) grated orange zest for the peanuts.

Nuts and Bolts

Makes about 12 cups (3 L)

Food writer Elizabeth Baird shared this easy recipe for a familiar crunchy snack she makes either with the traditional Worcestershire sauce flavouring or a Tex-Mex taste. Fill preserving jars with the mixture, tie with bright ribbon and present them as gifts.

....

3 cups (750 mL) cereal circles, such as Cheerios
3 cups (750 mL) mini wheat squares, such as Shreddies
2 cups (500 mL) dry roasted peanuts or mixed nuts

2 cups (500 mL) pretzel sticks
1 cup (250 mL) sesame sticks
1 cup (250 mL) mini snack crackers, such as Penguins or Goldfish

WORCESTERSHIRE SAUCE FLAVOURING
¾ cup (175 mL) butter
2 Tbsp (30 mL) Worcestershire sauce
½ tsp (2 mL) each celery salt, garlic salt and onion salt
½ tsp (2 mL) paprika

PREHEAT THE OVEN to 250°F (120°C).

In a large bowl, combine the round and square cereals, peanuts, pretzel and sesame sticks and snack crackers.

To make the Worcestershire Sauce Flavouring, microwave the butter with the Worcestershire sauce, celery salt, garlic salt, onion salt and paprika on low just until the butter has melted. Drizzle evenly over the cereal mixture, then toss to coat all the pieces.

Scrape the mixture into a large roasting pan. (A large foil roasting pan is ideal.) Bake in the centre of the oven for 1 to 1½ hours or until fragrant, slightly darkened and very crisp, stirring every 20 minutes. Let cool, then store in airtight containers for up to 2 weeks.

TEX-MEX NUTS AND BOLTS
Follow the recipe for Nuts and Bolts, substituting ¾ cup (175 mL) canola oil for melted butter, 1 Tbsp (15 mL) chili powder, 2 tsp (10 mL) garlic salt, ½ tsp (2 mL) each ground cumin and paprika and ¼ tsp (1 mL) hot pepper sauce for the Worcestershire Sauce Flavouring.

Cheering Drinks

ggnogs and assorted punches have always been popular for holiday entertaining. This rhyming recipe from 1853 for rum punch shows the simple origins of today's exotic Christmas drinks:

One sour,
Two sweet,
Four strong,
Eight weak.

A modern (delicious!) version of this would translate as "one part lemon juice, two parts sugar, four parts rum and eight parts water."

The recipes that follow reflect the sophisticated, yet easy-to-make holiday drinks now popular in Canadian homes.

Traditional Holiday Eggnog

Makes about 12 servings

Since this drink contains raw eggs, be sure you use only very fresh eggs and keep the eggnog cold at all times. If you are serving it for an open house, set its container in another, larger one of crushed ice.

....

6 eggs, separated
¼ tsp (1 mL) salt
⅔ cup (150 mL) powdered fruit sugar, divided

2½ cups (625 mL) half-and-half (10%) or table (18%) cream
1 cup (250 mL) milk
1 cup (250 mL) rum or brandy

1¼ cups (300 mL) whipping (35%) cream
Freshly grated nutmeg to taste

IN A LARGE BOWL, beat together the egg whites and salt until frothy. Gradually beat in half the sugar and continue beating until stiff peaks form.

In a separate large bowl, beat the egg yolks until light. Gradually add the remaining sugar, beating until thick and lemon-coloured.

Beating constantly, very slowly add the cream, milk and rum or brandy to the egg-yolk mixture.

In a medium bowl, whip the whipping cream until soft peaks form. Fold the whipped cream and stiff egg whites into the egg yolk mixture until well combined.

Cover and chill thoroughly. Ladle into glasses and sprinkle with nutmeg before serving.

Citrus-Rum Punch

Makes about 26 servings

Make your own blocks of ice for this zesty punch by freezing water
in milk cartons or large yogurt containers.

....

½ cup (125 mL) granulated
    sugar
¼ cup (60 mL) boiling water
3 cups (750 mL) golden rum
1 cup (250 mL) grapefruit
    juice

¾ cup (175 mL) frozen
    lemonade concentrate
¾ cup (175 mL) frozen orange
    concentrate

1 tsp (5 mL) orange bitters
5 cups (1.25 L) soda water
Lemon and orange slices

USING A MEASURING CUP, dissolve the
sugar in the boiling water. Cool.

In a large pitcher, combine the rum,
grapefruit juice, lemonade and orange juice
concentrates and orange bitters. Mix well.
Stir in the sugar syrup.

Just before serving, pour the rum
mixture over a block of ice in a large,
chilled punch bowl and add the soda water.
Stir gently. Garnish with lemon and orange
slices.

White Wine-Brandy Punch

Makes about 30 servings

This easy punch resembles a white wine sangria. For the mixture of winter fruit, choose a combination of peeled orange or grapefruit segments, lemon slices and/or fresh peeled and cored pineapple chunks.

....

1 cup (250 mL) prepared mixed winter fruit (see above)
1 cup (250 mL) brandy

3 bottles (750 mL each) chilled dry or medium-dry white wine

3 cups (750 mL) chilled soda water

PLACE THE FRUIT in a large punch bowl and add the brandy. Cover and refrigerate overnight.

Just before serving, place a large block of ice (see page 113 on how to make your own ice block) in the punch bowl and pour in the wine and soda water.

Cranberry Punch

Makes about 40 servings with gin; about 30 servings without gin

This colourful punch is refreshing and not overly sweet. Omit the gin for a non-alcoholic version. If you don't have a shallow ice-ring mould, use a Bundt or angel food pan with a hole in the centre, filling it only halfway with water after the initial freezing.

....

1 seedless orange
6 cups (1.5 L) cranberry cocktail
1 bottle (750 mL) gin (optional)

1½ cups (375 mL) frozen orange juice concentrate
¾ cup (175 mL) frozen lemonade concentrate
3 cups (750 mL) soda water

THINLY SLICE the orange and arrange the slices around the bottom of a ring mould. Pour in just enough water to cover the slices, then freeze until solid. Add enough cold water to fill the mould and freeze again.

In a large, chilled punch bowl, combine the cranberry cocktail, gin and orange juice and lemonade concentrates.

Just before serving, add the soda water. Unmould the orange ice ring by dipping it quickly into hot water. Float the ice ring in the punch.

Wassail Bowl

Makes about 12 servings

The custom of preparing a Wassail Bowl at Christmas came from the Saxons who drank from it to the toast of *waes hael*, meaning "good health." It was the traditional English "cup of cheer," and British settlers were quick to introduce it to Canada.

....

3 small apples, cored but
    unpeeled
3-inch (8 cm) cinnamon stick
2-inch (5 cm) piece dried
    ginger*
4 coriander seeds
3 whole cloves

3 whole allspice berries
2 cardamom pods
1 cup (250 mL) granulated
    sugar
1 cup (250 mL) water
½ tsp (2 mL) freshly grated
    nutmeg

¼ tsp (1 mL) ground mace
4½ cups (1.12 L) light ale
1 bottle (750 mL) dry sherry
    or Madeira
3 eggs, separated

PREHEAT THE OVEN to 350°F (180°C). Put the apples in a small baking dish and add water to a depth of ½ inch (1 cm). Cover tightly and bake for 30 to 45 minutes or until tender but not mushy.

Tie the cinnamon stick, ginger, coriander seeds, cloves, allspice berries and cardamom pods together in a piece of cheesecloth.

In a large non-reactive pot, combine the sugar and water. Add the spice bag, grated nutmeg and mace. Bring to a boil over high heat, stirring until the sugar has dissolved. Reduce the heat to medium-low and simmer, uncovered, for 10 minutes. Add the ale and sherry and reheat but do not allow to boil.

Just before serving, beat the egg whites until stiff in a medium bowl. In a large, heatproof punch bowl, beat the egg yolks until thick. Fold the whites into the yolks.

Remove the spice bag from the ale mixture and very gradually pour the ale mixture into the eggs, stirring briskly after each addition. Float the roasted apples on top of the punch. Serve hot.

* Look for pieces of dried ginger in Asian grocery stores.

Mulled Wine

Makes about 12 servings

The delightful fragrance of this hot drink will bring everyone into the kitchen, especially after a brisk session of neighbourhood carolling.

....

1 lemon
1 cup (250 mL) water
⅔ cup (150 mL) powdered fruit sugar

3-inch (8 cm) cinnamon stick
1 tsp (5 mL) whole cloves
¼ tsp (1 mL) freshly grated nutmeg

2 bottles (750 mL each) dry red wine
12 strips lemon peel

SLICE THE LEMON thinly and place in a small saucepan. Add the water, sugar and spices, and stir over medium heat until the sugar has dissolved and the mixture boils. Simmer for 10 minutes, stirring occasionally.

Pour the wine into a large non-reactive saucepan. Strain the sugar syrup into the wine, discarding the lemon slices and whole spices. Heat the wine mixture gently to the simmering point but do not allow it to boil. Ladle into heatproof glasses and serve hot garnished with strips of lemon peel.

SPICY WINE PUNCH To serve cold, strain the syrup into a 10-cup (2.5 L) pitcher. Add the wine and chill. Just before serving, add 1 cup (250 mL) chilled ginger ale or soda water. Garnish with strips of lemon peel.

Mulled Cider

Makes about 6 servings

Here's a warming festive beverage for all ages.

....

5 cups (1.25 L) fresh apple cider
¼ cup (60 mL) lightly packed brown sugar

¼ cup (60 mL) fresh lemon juice
4 whole cloves
1½-inch (4 cm) cinnamon stick

1½-inch (4 cm) piece dried ginger*
Freshly grated nutmeg to taste

IN A LARGE non-reactive saucepan, combine the cider, brown sugar and lemon juice. Heat the mixture slowly to simmering point but do not allow it to boil.

Meanwhile, tie the cloves, cinnamon stick and ginger together in a piece of cheesecloth. Add the bag of spices to the simmering liquid and heat over low heat for 15 minutes. Remove the spice bag. (You can prepare the mulled cider to this point and reheat it slowly before serving.) Ladle into heatproof glasses or mugs and serve hot garnished with a sprinkling of nutmeg.

* Look for pieces of dried ginger in Asian grocery stores.

OLD STONE FENCE Add 3 Tbsp (45 mL) of rum to each serving of Mulled Cider.

MULLED CRANBERRY-APPLE CIDER
Follow the recipe for Mulled Cider, substituting 3 cups (750 mL) fresh apple cider and 2 cups (500 mL) cranberry juice for the 5 cups (1.25 L) cider, and omitting the lemon juice.

Irish Coffee

Makes 1 serving

The holidays are a good excuse for this popular coffee.

....

| Powdered fruit sugar for rimming the glasses 1 tsp (5 mL) granulated sugar | ⅔ cup (150 mL) very hot strong black coffee | ¼ cup (60 mL) Irish whiskey 1 Tbsp (15 mL) whipped cream |

PUT THE POWDERED fruit sugar in a small dish. Rinse an 8 oz (250 mL) stemmed heatproof glass in very hot water. Invert the glass and shake it, then dip the rim of the glass in the dish of sugar.

Spoon the granulated sugar into the glass, leaving the spoon in the glass. Pour in the coffee and Irish whiskey, stirring to dissolve the sugar. Serve hot topped with whipped cream.

Holiday Feast Menus and Extras

hristmas always means lots of entertaining. To make the holidays more relaxing and fun, in this chapter I suggest menus for six special holiday feasts. Each menu features recipes from this book (see each menu for a list of recipes, with page references to the recipes; some are in this chapter and some you will find in other places in the book). And in the second part of the chapter (see pages 140 to 147) you will find a few extra recipes you might find handy over the holidays. Merry Christmas!

> ### Réveillon: A French-Canadian Christmas Eve Supper
>
> Mushroom Consommé (this page) Assorted pickles and relishes
> Tourtière (page 49) Dinner Rolls (page 91)
> Ragoût de Boulettes (facing page) Bûche de Noël (page 16)
> Tangy Cabbage Salad (page 122)

Mushroom Consommé

Makes 6 to 8 servings

This is a sophisticated way to begin a holiday meal. If you use canned consommé, dilute it according to the instructions on the can before measuring. The soup is delicious with white button mushrooms, but brown creminis are often the same price and have more flavour.
The soup can be made ahead up to the point of adding the sherry and lemon juice. Cover and refrigerate the soup for up to 2 days. Just before serving, add the sherry and lemon juice and reheat gently without boiling.

2 Tbsp (30 mL) butter
2 Tbsp (30 mL) minced green onion
1½ lb (750 g) brown cremini or white button mushrooms

6 cups (1.5 L) homemade beef stock or canned consommé (see note above)
1 cup (250 mL) dry sherry

1 tsp (5 mL) fresh lemon juice
Salt to taste
1 lemon, thinly sliced

HEAT THE BUTTER in a large saucepan and sauté the green onion for about 3 minutes or until translucent.

Mince the mushrooms in a food processor. (Alternatively, mince the mushrooms very finely with a sharp knife. Don't use a blender for this; it will turn the mushrooms to mush.) Add the mushrooms to the saucepan and cook for 5 minutes, stirring often.

Stir in the stock and bring to a boil. Reduce the heat and simmer, uncovered, for 30 minutes. Remove the saucepan from the heat and cool.

Strain the consommé through a sieve, pushing some of the mushroom pieces through the sieve into the consommé for texture.

Return the consommé to the rinsed-out saucepan. Add the sherry and lemon juice, and season with salt if necessary. Reheat slowly just to simmering point before serving. Garnish each serving with a thin slice of lemon.

Ragoût de Boulettes

(MEATBALL STEW)

Makes 6 servings

Making a broth with the pork hocks is well worth the effort for this delicious stew. As with any stew there is even more flavour if you make it a day or two ahead. Gently reheat on the stovetop or in a 350°F (180°C) oven for about 30 minutes or until bubbly and hot.

....

STEW
4 pork hocks
1 medium onion, peeled
6 whole cloves
1 stalk celery with leaves, diced
2 tsp (10 mL) salt
1 bay leaf
Freshly ground black pepper to taste
¼ cup (60 mL) butter

4 medium potatoes, peeled and quartered
1½ cups (375 mL) all-purpose flour

MEATBALLS
1½ lb (750 g) lean ground pork
½ cup (125 mL) fine dry breadcrumbs

½ cup (125 mL) finely chopped onion
1 egg, beaten
1 tsp (5 mL) salt
¼ tsp (1 mL) dry mustard
¼ tsp (1 mL) ground cloves
¼ tsp (1 mL) cinnamon
Freshly ground black pepper to taste
All-purpose flour for dusting

TO MAKE THE STEW, remove the skin from the pork hocks, place the pork hocks in a large pot and add enough cold water to just cover them. Bring to a boil and skim off any foam that appears on top.

Stud the whole onion with the cloves. Add the onion, celery, salt, bay leaf and pepper to the pot. Simmer, covered, for 2 hours.

Meanwhile, make the meatballs. In a large bowl, combine the ground pork, breadcrumbs, onion, egg, salt, mustard, cloves, cinnamon and pepper. Form the mixture into 1-inch (2.5 cm) balls. Place the meatballs in one layer on a baking sheet, cover loosely and refrigerate until the hocks have simmered for 2 hours.

When the hocks have cooked for 2 hours, melt the butter in a large heavy skillet. Dust the meatballs with flour, then add them to the skillet, in batches

if necessary, and brown them evenly on all sides.

Add the meatballs to the pot with the hocks and cook for 15 minutes. Add the potatoes and cook for 30 minutes longer or until the hocks are tender and the potatoes are tender but not mushy.

Remove the pork hocks from the liquid and cut off the meat in large pieces. Discard the bones and fat, and return the meat to the pot. Discard the bay leaf and whole onion studded with cloves.

In a large, clean skillet, brown the 1½ cups (375 mL) flour over medium heat, stirring until golden. Whisk in enough cold water to make a smooth, runny paste. Gradually add the flour paste to the stew and cook, stirring, for about 5 minutes after each addition to eliminate the starchy taste, until the stew is thickened to your liking.

Tangy Cabbage Salad

Makes at least 12 servings

This recipe makes a batch of delicious coleslaw that's large enough
to feed a holiday crowd. It keeps well for at least two weeks and, in fact,
is more flavourful if refrigerated for a day before serving.

COLESLAW
1 medium cabbage
1 cup (250 mL) seeded and
  chopped sweet green
  pepper
1 cup (250 mL) grated carrot
1 medium onion, chopped
1 Tbsp (15 mL) salt

Ice cubes
½ cup (125 mL) drained
  canned pimiento, chopped

DRESSING
1 cup (250 mL) granulated
  sugar
¾ cup (175 mL) white vinegar

½ cup (125 mL) canola oil
¼ cup (60 mL) water
1 tsp (5 mL) mustard seeds
1 tsp (5 mL) celery seeds

TO MAKE THE COLESLAW, shred the
cabbage by hand or in a food processor
fitted with the coarse shredding disc. In a
large bowl, toss the cabbage with the green
pepper, carrot, onion and salt. Cover with
ice cubes and let the mixture stand at room
temperature for at least 1 hour (this makes
the cabbage crisp). Drain well, return to the
bowl and add the pimiento.

To make the dressing, boil together the
sugar, vinegar, oil, water and mustard and
celery seeds in a small saucepan. Pour the
dressing over the cabbage mixture, toss
well then cool. Spoon into a large airtight
container, cover and refrigerate until ready
to serve.

A Traditional Christmas Dinner

Mushroom Consommé (page 120)

Roast Goose with Onion-Sage Dressing (page 124)

Giblet Gravy (page 125)

Spiced Apples (this page)

Red Cabbage with Apple (page 126)

Ginger-Glazed Carrots (page 127) or Fiddleheads (page 126)

Whipped Potato Casserole (page 127)

Steamed Carrot Pudding (page 26) with Fluffy White Pudding Sauce (page 35)

Spiced Nuts (page 107) and Candied Citrus Peel (page 104)

Spiced Apples

Makes 8 apple halves

Delicious on their own, these spiced apples also make a superb garnish for roast goose. Place a dab of redcurrant jelly in the hollow in each apple half and arrange them around the goose.

....

4 large tart apples

3 Tbsp (45 mL) fresh lemon juice

3 cups (750 mL) water

1½ cups (375 mL) granulated sugar

Cinnamon to taste

PREHEAT THE OVEN to 375°F (190°C). Peel, halve and core the apples. Sprinkle immediately with 2 Tbsp (30 mL) of the lemon juice.

In a large skillet, combine the water, sugar and remaining lemon juice and simmer, uncovered, for 5 minutes. Add the apple halves and poach them over medium heat, turning once, for 10 minutes or until barely tender but not soft.

Remove the apple halves with a slotted spoon and arrange, cut-side down, in a baking dish. Sprinkle with cinnamon.

Boil the syrup in the skillet over high heat until it has reduced to ½ cup (125 mL). Pour the syrup over the apples.

Bake, uncovered, for about 15 minutes, turning the apple halves once and basting with the syrup, until the apple halves are tender.

Roast Goose with Onion-Sage Dressing

Makes 8 servings

Geese provided a beautiful Christmas dinner long before people raised and ate turkey. Although very rich, a properly cooked goose is a grease-free treat. The dressing can be made a day ahead, cooled, covered and refrigerated, but don't stuff the goose until just before roasting it.

GOOSE
10 lb (5 kg) goose
Fresh lemon juice
Salt and freshly ground black pepper to taste
4 cups (1 L) boiling water or stock

ONION-SAGE DRESSING
½ cup (125 mL) dry red wine

¼ cup (60 mL) golden sultana raisins
½ cup (125 mL) butter
2 cups (500 mL) minced onions
1 large tart apple, peeled, cored and minced
1 cup (250 mL) minced celery with leaves
½ cup (125 mL) coarsely chopped pecans

6 cups (1.5 L) fresh breadcrumbs
1 tsp (5 mL) granulated sugar
1 tsp (5 mL) crumbled dried sage
½ tsp (2 mL) each crumbled dried savory, salt and freshly ground black pepper

FOR THE GOOSE, remove any loose fat from its cavity. Wipe and dry the goose thoroughly inside and out. Chop the liver and reserve it for the dressing. Reserve the neck, wing tips, gizzard and heart for the stock (see Giblet Gravy recipe on the facing page).

To make the dressing, combine the red wine and raisins in a small saucepan. Bring to a boil and boil for 3 minutes. Remove from the heat and cool. Drain the raisins, reserving the wine.

In a large skillet, melt the butter. Add the onions, apple and goose liver and sauté until the onion is translucent and the liver loses its pinkness. Add the celery and mix well. Remove the skillet from the heat and stir in the pecans and raisins.

In a large bowl, combine the breadcrumbs, sugar, sage, savory, salt and pepper. Stir in the onion mixture and cool.

Preheat the oven to 400°F (200°C). Rub the goose inside and out with lemon juice and sprinkle the inside with salt and pepper.

Stuff the neck cavity loosely with some of the dressing and fasten the neck skin to the body with a skewer. Stuff the body cavity loosely with the rest of the dressing, then tie or sew the opening shut. Tie the legs close to the body. Using a needle, prick the skin all over to allow the fat to escape.

Put the goose, breast-side down, on a rack in a shallow roasting pan. Pour 2 cups (500 mL) of the boiling water or stock over it (this helps remove the excess fat).

Roast, uncovered, for 20 minutes. Reduce the temperature to 325°F (160°C) and roast for 1 hour.

Reheat the reserved red wine until it is warm. Pour off the drippings that have accumulated in the roasting pan and baste the goose with some of the reserved wine. (Keep the wine warm for basting as the goose continues to cook.) Turn the goose onto its side and pour over the remaining boiling water or stock. Roast for another 30 minutes.

Pour off the drippings and baste again with some of the wine. Turn the goose onto its other side and roast for another 30 minutes.

Prick the goose again with the needle, pour off the drippings and baste with the remaining wine. Turn the goose onto its back and roast for 1½ hours. The total roasting time will be 3½ to 4 hours and a meat thermometer inserted into the thickest part of the thigh should register 180°F (82°C).

Remove the goose from the oven and let it rest for 15 minutes in a warm place so that the juices are reabsorbed. Spoon out the dressing, carve the goose and serve.

Giblet Gravy

Makes 0 servings

For flavour, nothing beats gravy made from the giblets of the bird. Make the giblet stock on Christmas Eve to make the big day more relaxing. If you wish, you can use only the stock for gravy and put the chopped, cooked giblets to another use.

GIBLET STOCK
Reserved giblets (neck, wing tips, gizzard and heart) from a goose or turkey
1 small onion, coarsely chopped
1 stalk celery with leaves
1 carrot, coarsely chopped
1 large sprig parsley
4 whole black peppercorns
½ tsp (2 mL) dried thyme leaves
½ tsp (2 mL) salt

GRAVY
3 cups (750 mL) giblet stock
¼ cup (60 mL) cold water
2 Tbsp (30 mL) cornstarch
Salt and freshly ground black pepper to taste

TO MAKE THE STOCK, put the giblets in a medium saucepan and enough cold water to just cover them. Bring to a boil and skim off any foam. Add the onion, celery, carrot, parsley, peppercorns, thyme and salt. Bring to a boil again, then reduce the heat and simmer, covered, for about 2 hours. Remove the giblets and reserve. Strain the liquid, discarding the vegetables and peppercorns. Chop the giblets, cover and refrigerate.

To make the gravy, skim any excess fat from the drippings left in the roasting pan after the bird is done. Pour the giblet stock into the roasting pan with the remaining drippings and heat, stirring to scrape up the browned bits from the bottom of the pan.

In a small bowl, stir together the water and cornstarch until smooth and add to the pan, stirring constantly. Simmer the gravy for about 5 minutes or until smooth and thick. To thicken the gravy more, stir together more water and cornstarch and add to the gravy; to thin it, gradually stir in more hot stock or hot water.

Add salt and pepper to taste. Stir in the cooked giblets and heat through. Serve in a warm gravy boat.

Red Cabbage with Apple

Makes 6 servings

Red cabbage is the traditional accompaniment to roast goose and, since its flavour improves with reheating, the red cabbage can be prepared days in advance.

....

2 lb (1 kg) red cabbage
2 medium apples
¼ cup (60 mL) lard
½ cup (125 mL) finely chopped onion

¼ cup (60 mL) boiling water
¼ cup (60 mL) red wine vinegar
2 Tbsp (30 mL) granulated sugar

1 tsp (5 mL) salt
1 small bay leaf
¼ tsp (1 mL) ground cloves

REMOVE THE TOUGH outer leaves of the cabbage, cut the cabbage into quarters and remove the core. Shred the cabbage by hand or in a food processor fitted with the coarse shredding disc. Peel, core and chop the apples.

Heat the lard in a large skillet or saucepan. Add the apples and onion and cook, stirring, for 5 minutes or until the onion is translucent.

Add the cabbage, water, vinegar, sugar, salt, bay leaf and ground cloves. Bring to a boil, then reduce the heat and cook, covered and stirring often, for about 45 minutes, or until the cabbage is very tender. Check during cooking time to make sure the cabbage is moist and add a bit more water if needed. Remove the bay leaf before serving.

Fiddleheads

Fiddleheads or ferns are a specialty of New Brunswick, but they are found in other provinces as well. I'm including them here because they are a special treat in our family. My husband gathers them in the spring when we enjoy them fresh, then we freeze a few packages to savour throughout the year, always reserving one package for our Christmas dinner.

Steam fresh fiddleheads for about 8 minutes or until tender but still crisp. If fresh fiddleheads aren't available, use frozen ones and follow the instructions on the package; you'll need two 300 g packages for six to eight people. Either way, serve the fiddleheads with butter, lemon juice, salt and pepper to taste.

Ginger-Glazed Carrots

Makes 6 servings

Root vegetables like carrots were prominent in early Canadian
holiday feasts because they kept so well into the winter.

....

1 lb (500 g) carrots
¼ cup (60 mL) butter

2 Tbsp (30 mL) lightly packed
   brown sugar
1 tsp (5 mL) ground ginger

Salt and freshly ground black
   pepper to taste
Minced parsley for garnish

PEEL THE CARROTS and cut into
matchsticks. In a heavy skillet, melt the
butter and add the carrots. Cover with a
sheet of buttered wax or parchment paper,
then with a lid. Steam over low heat for
10 to 12 minutes or until just tender.

Remove the lid and paper. Sprinkle
with brown sugar, ginger and salt and
pepper. Cook, stirring frequently, for
another 2 minutes or until glazed. Garnish
with parsley.

Whipped Potato Casserole

Makes 10 servings

It is difficult to prepare fluffy mashed potatoes ahead of time, but this
delicious casserole provides an easy solution to the problem.

....

10 to 12 medium potatoes
⅓ cup (75 mL) butter, divided
1 pkg (250 g) block cream
   cheese, cubed

1 cup (250 mL) sour cream
Salt and freshly ground black
   pepper

¼ cup (60 mL) fine dry
   breadcrumbs

GREASE A 2-quart (2 L) casserole. Cook the
potatoes, covered, in boiling salted water for
20 to 30 minutes or until tender. Drain and
return to the saucepan over low heat briefly
to dry.

Mash the potatoes with ¼ cup (60 mL)
of the butter. Add the cream cheese, sour
cream and salt and pepper to taste. Beat
until creamy, but do not over-beat or the
potatoes will become gluey. Spoon the
potatoes into the prepared casserole.

Melt the remaining butter and combine
with the breadcrumbs in a small bowl.
Sprinkle evenly on top of the potatoes.
Refrigerate, covered, for up to 2 days.

Remove the casserole from the
refrigerator 30 minutes before reheating in
a 350°F (180°C) oven. Bake the potatoes
for about 30 minutes or until hot
throughout.

An Early Canadian Christmas Dinner

Traditional Holiday Eggnog (page 112)
Maple-Glazed Stuffed Pork (this page)
Baked Cranberry Sauce (facing page)
Rice-Mushroom Ring (page 130) filled
 with buttered green peas

Rutabaga Puff (page 131)
Pumpkin Pie (page 44) and
 whipped cream

Maple-Glazed Stuffed Pork

Makes 8 servings

Before they had enough land cleared to allow them to keep cattle,
early Canadian settlers raised pigs that could thrive on kitchen scraps.
Canadian pork is still considered among the world's best, and a pork roast
is high on my list when I entertain.

¼ cup (60 mL) butter
1 cup (250 mL) chopped
 celery
1 cup (250 mL) finely diced
 mushrooms
½ cup (125 mL) chopped
 onion
1 cup (250 mL) fine dry
 breadcrumbs
1 tsp (5 mL) salt
½ tsp (2 mL) grated orange
 zest

½ tsp (2 mL) dried crushed
 basil
¼ tsp (1 mL) dried thyme
 leaves
¼ tsp (1 mL) crumbled dried
 sage
¼ cup (60 mL) chopped
 parsley
¼ tsp (1 mL) freshly ground
 black pepper

4 lb (1.8 kg) long, narrow
 boneless double pork loin
 roast*
1 cup (250 mL) dry white
 wine or chicken stock
1 orange, thinly sliced
½ cup (125 mL) maple syrup
½ cup (125 mL) orange juice
Parsley sprigs for garnish

MELT THE BUTTER in a large skillet. Add
the celery, mushrooms and onion, and sauté
until the onion is translucent. Remove
the skillet from the heat. Stir in the
breadcrumbs, salt, orange zest, herbs and
pepper.

Preheat the oven to 325°F (160°C). Snip
the strings on the roast and open it up like
a book. Pat and mound the stuffing evenly
over the inside surface of half the roast.
Replace the other half of the roast and

tie tightly with kitchen string at 1-inch
(2.5 cm) intervals. Place the roast on a rack
in a shallow roasting pan and pour the wine
into the pan. Roast for 1½ to 2 hours or
until a meat thermometer inserted into the
roast registers 155°F (68°C).

Thirty minutes before the pork is ready,
add the orange slices to the roasting pan.
Combine the maple syrup and orange juice
in a small bowl, and baste the pork with
the maple syrup mixture every 15 minutes

during the last 30 minutes of roasting.

Transfer the roast to a cutting board and tent with foil. Let it rest for 15 minutes or until a clean meat thermometer inserted into the roast registers 160°F (70°C). Slice the pork and serve garnished with the orange slices and lots of fresh parsley.

* A boneless double pork loin roast comprises two boneless loins tied together to make a nice even-sized roast. If you don't see one on your supermarket's meat counter, ask your butcher to tie one for you.

Baked Cranberry Sauce

Makes 1⅓ cups (325 mL)

This easy classic is delicious with roast turkey, pork, goose and duck.

2 cups (500 mL) fresh or frozen cranberries*

1 cup (250 mL) lightly packed brown sugar

¼ tsp (1 mL) ground cloves

PREHEAT THE OVEN to 350°F (180°C). Rinse and drain the cranberries and place them in a 4-cup (1 L) baking dish. Sprinkle the brown sugar and cloves over the cranberries. Cover and bake for 30 minutes, stirring occasionally.

* If using frozen cranberries, there's no need to thaw them first.

Rice-Mushroom Ring

Makes about 6 servings

This easy-to-make side looks pretty served with bright green
vegetables in the centre.

....

¼ cup (60 mL) butter
1 cup (250 mL) sliced
  mushrooms
½ cup (125 mL) blanched
  slivered almonds

2 Tbsp (30 mL) sherry
2½ cups (625 mL) cooked
  wild rice (see below), white
  or brown rice

Freshly grated nutmeg to
  taste

GREASE A 4-cup (1 L) tube pan with butter.
Preheat the oven to 350°F (180°C).

Melt the butter in a large skillet and
sauté the mushrooms for 2 to 3 minutes or
until slightly coloured. Stir in the almonds
and sherry. Remove the skillet from the
heat.

Put the rice in a large bowl, then
sprinkle with nutmeg. Add the mushroom
mixture and combine well. Pack into the
prepared pan. (The ring can be refrigerated
at this point, if you wish. Bring it back to
room temperature before baking.)

Set the pan in a shallow pan of hot
water and bake for 20 minutes or until
heated through.

To serve, loosen the ring by running a
sharp, thin knife around the edge. Invert
the ring onto a warm platter by placing
the platter over the top of the mould, then
turning over the two together and carefully
removing the ring. Serve hot.

HOW TO COOK WILD RICE

Wash ⅔ cup (150 mL) raw wild rice and
soak it for several hours in cold water.
Wash the rice again, changing the water
once or twice. Stir the washed rice into
3 cups (750 mL) boiling water. Reduce the
heat to medium-low and cook, covered, for
20 minutes or until the wild rice is tender.
(If you prefer, skip the soaking step and
cook the rice for about 35 minutes.)

Rutabaga Puff

Makes 6 to 8 servings

For the smoothest, fluffiest rutabaga, use a food processor to purée it before adding the remaining ingredients. You can make, cover and refrigerate this traditional side a day or two in advance. Bring to room temperature before reheating and allow a few minutes longer.

3 cups (750 mL) hot, mashed rutabaga (1 medium-to-large rutabaga)
2 Tbsp (30 mL) butter
2 eggs, beaten
3 Tbsp (45 mL) all-purpose flour

1 Tbsp (15 mL) firmly packed brown sugar
1 tsp (5 mL) baking powder
1 tsp (5 mL) salt
Freshly ground black pepper to taste

Freshly grated nutmeg to taste
¼ cup (60 mL) fine dry breadcrumbs
1 Tbsp (15 mL) butter, melted

GREASE A 6-cup (1.5 L) casserole with butter. Preheat the oven to 375°F (190°C).

In a food processor, combine the hot, mashed rutabaga, butter and eggs, and process until smooth. Add the flour, sugar, baking powder, salt, pepper and nutmeg, and process until well blended. (Alternatively, mash the rutabaga with a potato masher until smooth, then add the remaining ingredients and combine well.) Spoon the rutabaga mixture into the prepared casserole.

In a small bowl, combine the breadcrumbs and melted butter and sprinkle evenly over the rutabaga mixture. Bake, uncovered, for about 25 minutes or until lightly browned.

A Holiday Brunch

Winter Fruit Salad (page 33) and
   Creamy Dressing (page 37)
Brie and Prosciutto Bread Pudding
   (facing page)

Glazed Peameal Bacon Roast
   (this page)
Butter Kringle (page 86)

Glazed Peameal Bacon Roast

Makes 8 servings

Glazed peameal bacon provides a delicious main course for a holiday brunch. Try this with the Tangy Cranberry Relish on page 137.

2 lb (1 kg) centre-cut peameal
   bacon roast
½ cup (125 mL) lightly packed
   brown sugar

2 Tbsp (30 mL) all-purpose
   flour
½ tsp (2 mL) dry mustard
⅛ tsp (0.5 mL) ground cloves

½ cup (125 mL) apple cider
1 Tbsp (15 mL) cider vinegar

PREHEAT THE OVEN to 325°F (160°C). Place the bacon roast in a shallow baking pan. In a small bowl, combine the brown sugar, flour, mustard and cloves, then gradually stir in the apple cider and vinegar.

Spread the brown sugar mixture over the bacon.

Bake for 1 hour, basting every 15 minutes with the glaze that's accumulated in the pan. Serve hot, cut into slices.

Brie and Prosciutto Bread Pudding

Makes 6 to 8 servings

Bread puddings were originally made by frugal cooks who wanted to avoid wasting stale bread. Popular still, they take on all sorts of delicious forms. One version is a breakfast dish, often called a strata because the bread is layered with a savoury custard, plus cheese and other ingredients such as ham or sausage. In community cookbooks that popped up in the 1950s, the pudding was sometimes called "Wife Saver" because it's made the day before, thus saving "the wife" from having to cook in the early morning—a special treat for a day like Christmas Day.

Whether you make this for Christmas brunch or overnight company through the year, you'll discover why bread puddings have become a national treat. Try to find egg bread for this since it melds into the custard and melted cheese in an especially yummy way, even with the crust left on.

....

10 to 12 slices egg bread
¼ cup (60 mL) butter, melted
4 oz (125 g) prosciutto, slivered
8 oz (250 g) brie cheese, rind removed and cut into cubes

1 cup (250 mL) grated old cheddar cheese
6 eggs
3 cups (750 mL) milk
¼ cup (60 mL) minced shallots

1 Tbsp (15 mL) Dijon mustard
½ tsp (2 mL) each salt and freshly ground black pepper
Dash each Tabasco and Worcestershire sauces
1 tsp (5 mL) paprika

LINE A GREASED 13- × 9-inch (3 L) baking dish with half of the bread, cutting it to fit. Brush the bread with half of the butter. Sprinkle with half of the prosciutto and half of the brie and cheddar. Repeat the layers.

In a large bowl, whisk the eggs, then whisk in the milk, shallots, mustard, salt, pepper, Tabasco and Worcestershire sauces. Pour the egg mixture over the bread, then cover and refrigerate overnight.

When ready to bake, preheat the oven to 350°F (180°C). Sprinkle the top of the pudding with paprika, then bake, uncovered, for about 1 hour or until puffed and crisp on top. Cut into squares to serve.

Scalloped Oysters

Makes 6 servings

When chatting with oyster farmers in Scotland, I discovered oysters
at Christmas were a British tradition that has since died out,
but the farmers were interested to know Canadians carry it on,
thanks to Scottish settlers. Our family serves oysters on the half shell
on Christmas Eve each year, and enjoys them in a hearty stew,
like this one, at some point over the holidays.

¼ cup (60 mL) butter
3 Tbsp (45 mL) chopped
  green onion
2 Tbsp (30 mL) diced celery
3 Tbsp (45 mL) all-purpose
  flour
¼ tsp (1 mL) salt

¼ tsp (1 mL) freshly ground
  black pepper
⅛ tsp (0.5 mL) cayenne
¾ cup (175 mL) whole
  (3.25%) milk
½ cup (125 mL) whipping
  (35%) cream

1½ cups (375 mL) fine cracker
  crumbs
2 cups (500 mL) shucked
  oysters and their liquid
Paprika for dusting

GREASE A 6-cup (1.5 L) casserole with
butter. Preheat the oven to 400°F (200°C).

In a medium skillet, melt the butter and
sauté the onion and celery until the onion
is translucent. Add the flour, salt, pepper
and cayenne. Cook, stirring, for 2 minutes.
Remove the skillet from the heat.

In a small saucepan, heat the milk and
cream together until lukewarm. Gradually
add this to the onion mixture, stirring
constantly and cooking until thickened.

Place one-third of the crumbs in the
prepared casserole and cover with half of
the oysters and their liquid and half of the
onion mixture. Cover with another third of
the crumbs. Top with the remaining oysters
and liquid, then onion mixture, ending
with the remaining crumbs. (There should
be no more than two layers of oysters.)

Dust the top with a very light sprinkling
of paprika, then bake for 20 to 30 minutes
or until bubbly and brown.

Spiced Beef

Makes 12 servings

Wherever the Irish have settled in Canada, spiced beef is a favourite, especially at Christmas. It's easy to prepare and keeps for weeks.

....

3 Tbsp (45 mL) whole mixed pickling spice
4 cloves garlic
4 dried red chilies

2½ tsp (12 mL) salt
1 tsp (5 mL) granulated sugar
1 tsp (5 mL) saltpetre*
¼ tsp (1 mL) cinnamon

¼ tsp (1 mL) ground allspice
¼ tsp (1 mL) ground mace
5 lb (2.2 kg) boneless inside or outside round beef roast

PLACE ALL THE INGREDIENTS, except the beef, in a blender, food processor or mini-chopper and blend until a fine powder forms. (Alternatively, pound the ingredients in a mortar and pestle.) Rub the powder evenly into the meat on all sides.

Wrap the meat tightly in heavy-duty foil and place it on a platter in the refrigerator for 10 to 14 days, turning occasionally.

When ready to cook, preheat the oven to 225°F (110°C). Leaving the meat wrapped in the foil, place it in a shallow roasting pan and roast for 7 hours. Make certain the roast remains tightly wrapped while it's roasting.

Cool completely in the foil, then unwrap and scrape off most of the outside mixture before slicing the meat into thin slices.

* Saltpetre is the common name for potassium nitrate. In this recipe it's used to help preserve the beef and retain its colour. Saltpetre is increasingly hard to find; check with your pharmacy for a possible source. If unavailable, substitute coarse sea salt which, with the table salt, will provide preservation qualities, but perhaps not the colour retention.

Pickled Mushrooms

Makes about 2½ cups (625 mL)

Years ago in Ukrainian-Canadian homes, wild mushrooms
were pickled for special winter meals. Today, although mushrooms
are readily available, these delicacies are still enjoyed on Ukrainian
Christmas Eve (January 6), but also make a nice addition to any selection
of appetizers throughout the year.

MUSHROOMS
1 lb (500 g) small white
    button mushrooms
1½ cups (375 mL) white
    vinegar
1½ cups (375 mL) hot water
1 bay leaf

PICKLING MIXTURE
¼ cup (60 mL) canola oil
2 cloves garlic, halved
2 tsp (10 mL) salt
1 tsp (5 mL) whole black
    peppercorns
½ tsp (2 mL) ground mace

¼ tsp (1 mL) hot pepper
    flakes
⅔ cup (150 mL) white vinegar
    (approx.)

FOR THE MUSHROOMS, clean them and
place in a non-reactive saucepan. Add the
white vinegar, hot water and bay leaf. Bring
to a boil, then reduce the heat and simmer,
uncovered, for 5 minutes. Drain, discarding
the liquid and bay leaf. Cool, then pack in a
4-cup (1 L) glass jar.

To make the pickling mixture, mix
together the oil, garlic, salt, peppercorns,
mace and hot pepper flakes in a small bowl,
stirring until the salt dissolves. Pour the
oil mixture over the mushrooms, then add
enough vinegar to cover the mushrooms,
but no more than ⅔ cup (150 mL). Cover
tightly and refrigerate for 2 or 3 days before
using. Serve cold and well drained.

A New Year's Dinner

Mulled Wine (page 116)

Potted Cheese (page 97) and Herb
　Batter Bread (page 92)

Tangy Cranberry Relish (this page)

Roast Duck with Apricot-Rice
　Dressing and Pan Gravy (page 138)

Breaded Parsnips (page 139)

Lemony Brussels Sprouts
　(page 139)

Steamed Fig Pudding (page 27) and
　Foamy Orange Sauce (page 37)

Irish Coffee (page 117)

Tangy Cranberry Relish

Makes about 3½ cups (875 mL)

This uncooked relish is good with roast turkey and pork, too.

2 cups (500 mL) fresh or
　frozen cranberries*

1 orange

½ lemon

1 cup (250 mL) granulated
　sugar

½ cup (125 mL) golden
　sultana raisins

½ cup (125 mL) chopped
　walnuts

1 tsp (5 mL) ground cloves

IN A FOOD PROCESSOR, process the cranberries until minced. (Alternatively, mince the cranberries very finely with a sharp knife. Don't use a blender for this; it will turn the cranberries to mush.) Tip the cranberries into a 4-cup (1 L) non-reactive bowl.

With a small, sharp knife, remove the zest from the orange and lemon half and set aside. Peel off the white pith and discard. Cut the orange and lemon flesh into sections, discarding the seeds.

Process the rind and flesh in the food processor until minced, then add to the cranberries. (Alternatively, mince the rind and flesh very finely with a sharp knife. Don't use a blender for this; it will turn the rind and flesh to mush.) Add the sugar and stir well to dissolve. Thoroughly mix in the remaining ingredients.

Cover and refrigerate overnight so the flavours can mingle. The relish will keep for about a week in the refrigerator and freezes well, too.

* If using frozen cranberries, there's no need to thaw them first.

Roast Duck with Apricot-Rice Dressing and Pan Gravy

Makes 4 servings

Browning the duck before stuffing it eliminates the grease in the dressing.

....

DUCK
5 lb (2.2 kg) duck
Salt and freshly ground black pepper to taste
½ cup (125 mL) chicken stock
½ cup (125 mL) dry white wine

APRICOT-RICE DRESSING
¼ cup (60 mL) butter
¼ cup (60 mL) chopped onion
¼ cup (60 mL) chopped celery
⅔ cup (150 mL) brown rice
½ cup (125 mL) sliced mushrooms
½ tsp (2 mL) crumbled dried savory
½ tsp (2 mL) salt
¼ tsp (1 mL) freshly ground black pepper
1½ cups (375 mL) chicken stock (approx.)

1 cup (250 mL) diced dried apricots
¼ cup (60 mL) chopped pecans

PAN GRAVY
2 Tbsp (30 mL) cold water
2 tsp (10 mL) cornstarch
Canned apricots, drained and sliced, for garnish
Watercress for garnish

PREHEAT THE OVEN to 450°F (230°C).

Wipe the duck and dry thoroughly inside and out. Rub the skin with salt and pepper, then place on a rack in a shallow roasting pan. Using a needle, prick the skin all over to allow the fat to escape. Roast, uncovered, for 30 minutes or until the skin is well browned.

Transfer to a large ovenproof casserole and set aside. Discard the fat from the roasting pan, keeping any browned bits in the pan. Reduce the oven temperature to 325°F (160°C).

To make the dressing, melt the butter in a large skillet. Add the onion and celery and sauté until the onion is translucent. Add the brown rice, mushrooms and seasonings and cook over low heat, stirring occasionally, until the rice starts to brown.

Add enough stock to just cover the rice, and stir in the apricots. Cover and simmer for 35 to 40 minutes or until the stock has been absorbed. Add the pecans and cool.

Stuff the browned duck loosely with the dressing, then truss and tie securely. Return the duck to the casserole.

Add the chicken stock and wine to the reserved roasting pan. Bring to a boil, scraping up all the browned bits and pour the mixture over the duck. Cover the casserole and roast for 1½ hours or until a meat thermometer inserted in the thickest part of the thigh registers 180°F (82°C). Transfer the duck to a hot platter, cover loosely and keep warm.

To make the pan gravy, skim off the excess fat from the casserole. In a small bowl, stir together the cold water and cornstarch until smooth, then stir gradually into the pan drippings. Simmer, stirring often, for 5 minutes.

Serve the duck hot with the pan gravy and dressing garnished with apricots and watercress.

Lemony Brussels Sprouts

Makes 6 servings

Don't overcook these tiny, elegant members of the cabbage family.

....

4 cups (1 L) Brussels sprouts
Ice water
2 cups (500 mL) chicken
   stock

¼ cup (60 mL) butter
1½ Tbsp (22 mL) fresh lemon
   juice

Salt and freshly ground black
   pepper to taste

CUT THE ROOT END off each sprout and remove any damaged outer leaves. Soak the Brussels sprouts in a bowl of ice water for 1 hour. Drain.

In a large saucepan, bring the chicken stock to a boil. Add the sprouts and cook, covered, for 10 to 15 minutes (depending on size) or until just tender but still bright green. Drain and discard the stock.

Meanwhile, melt the butter in a small saucepan. Remove from the heat and add the lemon juice. Put the Brussels sprouts in a warm serving dish and pour over the lemon butter. Season with salt and pepper to taste.

Breaded Parsnips

Makes 6 servings

Among Canada's sweetest vegetables, parsnips are delicious under a crisp crumb coating. Try them, too, with roast pork.

....

1 lb (500 g) parsnips
1 egg
2 Tbsp (30 mL) milk
½ cup (125 mL) fine dry
   breadcrumbs

½ tsp (2 mL) salt
¼ tsp (1 mL) crumbled dried
   savory

Freshly ground black pepper
   to taste
¼ cup (60 mL) butter

PEEL THE PARSNIPS and cut them into large pieces about 2½ inches (6 cm) long. Cook in a saucepan of boiling salted water for 8 to 10 minutes or until almost tender. Drain.

In a shallow dish, beat the egg and milk together. In a second shallow dish, toss the breadcrumbs with the salt, savory and pepper.

Melt the butter in a heavy skillet. Dip each piece of parsnip in the egg mixture, then in the crumbs. Cook in the butter until golden brown, turning often.

Clam Chowder

Makes 6 servings

This chowder from Nova Scotia is a hearty offering
for guests at a tree-trimming party.

···

½ cup (125 mL) diced salt
  pork
1 large onion, minced
1 cup (250 mL) diced celery
1 cup (250 mL) peeled diced
  potatoes

1 cup (250 mL) diced carrots
1 can (10 oz/84 g) clams
1 can (19 oz/540 mL) diced
  tomatoes, with their juice
1½ tsp (7 mL) salt (or to
  taste)

¼ tsp (1 mL) dried thyme
  leaves
Whipping (35%) cream to
  serve

COOK THE SALT PORK in a large saucepan
over low heat until it is crisp and brown.
Add the vegetables and cook, stirring,
for 5 to 8 minutes or until the onion is
translucent.

Meanwhile, drain the clams, reserving
the clams and juice separately. Add the
clam juice, tomatoes with their juice,

salt and thyme to the saucepan. Bring to
a boil, then reduce the heat to low and
simmer, covered, for 30 minutes or until the
vegetables are tender.

Add the clams to the chowder and heat
through but do not boil. Serve the chowder
with a jug of cold whipping cream so that
each person can add it to taste.

Creamed Cod au Gratin

Makes 6 servings

Creamed cod is traditionally served by Maritimers on Boxing Day as a
welcome change from the heavy, rich meals of Christmas.

···

1½ lb (750 g) cod fillets
2 cups (500 mL) milk
3 Tbsp (45 mL) butter
¼ cup (60 mL) all-purpose
  flour

½ tsp (2 mL) dry mustard
½ tsp (2 mL) salt
Freshly ground black pepper
  to taste

1 cup (250 mL) grated old
  cheddar cheese
¼ cup (60 mL) fine dry
  breadcrumbs

GREASE A 9-inch (2.5 L) square baking
dish. Preheat the oven to 350°F (180°C).

In a large, deep skillet, simmer the fish
in the milk, covered, for about 10 minutes

per 1 inch (2.5 cm) of thickness or until
the fish flakes easily with a fork. Drain and
reserve the fish and milk separately. Flake
the fish and put it in the prepared dish.

In a medium saucepan, melt the butter over medium heat. Add the flour and cook, stirring, for 2 to 3 minutes. Remove from the heat and gradually stir in the reserved warm milk. Return the saucepan to the heat and cook, stirring, until thick and smooth. Stir in the mustard, salt and pepper. Pour the sauce over the fish.

In a small bowl, mix together the cheese and breadcrumbs and sprinkle over the fish and sauce. Place the baking dish in a shallow pan containing ¼ inch (6 mm) hot water. Bake for 25 minutes or until the cheese has melted and the cod mixture is piping hot.

Creamy Scrambled Eggs

Makes 4 to 6 servings

Adding cream cheese to these scrambled eggs means they stay creamy longer, so are perfect for a company brunch. If you have a chafing dish, you can cook the eggs right in the dish.

6 eggs
¼ cup (60 mL) half-and-half (10%) or table (18%) cream

¼ cup (60 mL) dry white wine
½ tsp (2 mL) salt
Freshly ground black pepper to taste

2 Tbsp (30 mL) butter
4 oz (125 g) block cream cheese, cubed

IN A MEDIUM BOWL, beat the eggs lightly. Add the cream, wine, salt and pepper.

Melt the butter in the top half of a double boiler or in a heatproof bowl set over a saucepan of simmering water. Pour in the egg mixture. Cook, stirring occasionally, over medium-low heat until the eggs are almost firm but still very moist. Stir in the cream cheese until it melts and blends. Serve hot.

Roast Turkey with Sausage Dressing

Makes 12 to 15 servings with leftovers

Turkey became a popular Christmas main course in Canada as early as the 19th century. Today, it is often served throughout the rest of the year as well.

Although pre-basted turkeys are available, it is much more economical to baste the turkey with butter yourself as it roasts. The sausage meat dressing in this recipe will add moisture to the meat as well. Serve this with Giblet Gravy (page 125) and Baked Cranberry Sauce (page 129) or Tangy Cranberry Relish (page 137).

....

1 lb (500 g) bulk sausage meat	8 cups (2 L) cubed day-old bread	½ tsp (2 mL) freshly ground black pepper
½ cup (125 mL) chopped onion	1 tsp (5 mL) granulated sugar	12 to 15 lb (5.5 to 6.7 kg) turkey (see Turkey Tips below)
½ cup (125 mL) diced celery	1 tsp (5 mL) crumbled dried sage	
¼ cup (60 mL) minced parsley	1 tsp (5 mL) salt	½ cup (125 mL) butter, softened

TO MAKE THE DRESSING, sauté the sausage meat in a heavy skillet, stirring frequently, until no sign of pink remains. Add the onion, celery and parsley and sauté until the onion is translucent. Drain the excess fat from the pan and set the mixture aside to cool.

Place the bread cubes in a large bowl and mix in the sugar, sage, salt and pepper. Add the sausage mixture and combine well.

Preheat the oven to 325°F (160°C). Wipe off the turkey and dry it thoroughly inside and out. Reserve the neck and giblets for stock.

Sprinkle the inside of the turkey with salt and pepper. Stuff the neck cavity loosely with some of the dressing and fasten the neck skin to the body with a skewer. Stuff the body cavity loosely with the rest of the dressing and tie or sew it shut. Tie the legs and wings close to the body.

Spread the butter over the skin. Place the turkey, breast side up, on a rack in a shallow roasting pan. Tent the bird with foil, tucking in the sides but leaving the ends open.

Roast for 3 hours, basting with the pan juices every 30 minutes. Uncover the turkey and roast for another 1 to 1½ hours, basting every 30 minutes, until a meat thermometer inserted in the thickest part of the thigh registers 180°F (82°C) and the juices run clear when you insert a skewer in the thickest part of the thigh.

Let the turkey rest, loosely covered with foil, for 20 to 30 minutes in a warm place so that the juices are reabsorbed. Remove the dressing before carving.

TURKEY TIPS If you can't find a fresh turkey, thaw a frozen bird in the refrigerator, allowing 6 hours per pound

(500 g) and remembering it can take several days to thaw a large turkey.

The dressing (stuffing) can be made a day ahead, then cooled, covered and refrigerated, but don't stuff the turkey until just before roasting.

Remember to baste a roasting turkey often because the meat is drier than that of goose or duck.

As new breeds of turkey are developed, roasting times are decreasing. Normally, turkey should take about 20 minutes per pound (500 g). Don't be surprised if your bird is done sooner; just let it rest in a warm place, loosely covered with foil.

Brandied Cranberries

Makes about 4 cups (1 L)

Serve this brandy-spiked sauce with roast turkey, duck or goose.

....

1½ cups (375 mL) granulated sugar
2 Tbsp (30 mL) grated orange zest
½ cup (125 mL) orange juice

½ cup (125 mL) water
¼ cup (60 mL) brandy
4 cups (1 L) fresh or frozen cranberries*

2 Tbsp (30 mL) redcurrant jelly
1 tsp (5 mL) ground ginger

IN A LARGE heavy-bottomed saucepan, combine the sugar, orange zest and juice, water and brandy. Bring to a boil, stirring until the sugar has dissolved.

Add the cranberries and bring back to a boil. Continue boiling, stirring constantly, for about 5 minutes or until the skins pop.

Remove from the heat and stir in the redcurrant jelly and ginger. Cover and refrigerate. Serve cold.

* If using frozen cranberries, there's no need to thaw them first.

Ham Cooked in Beer

Makes 10 to 12 servings

Choose a smoked ham on the bone for the best flavour. Here it's heated in beer, then glazed in a lovely maple mixture.

....

5 lb (2.2 kg) cooked smoked ham
1½ cups (375 mL) lager
Whole cloves for studding
½ cup (125 mL) lightly packed brown sugar
¼ cup (60 mL) maple syrup
2 Tbsp (30 mL) all-purpose flour
2 tsp (10 mL) dry mustard
Canned peach halves for garnish
Parsley for garnish

PLACE THE HAM in a large saucepan and pour in enough water to almost cover it. Add the beer and bring to a boil. Reduce the heat to low and simmer, partially covered, for 2 hours. Preheat the oven to 350°F (180°C).

Drain the ham, discarding the liquid. Place the ham, fat side up, on a rack in a shallow roasting pan. If there is skin on the ham, remove it. Using a sharp knife, score the fat into diamond shapes, then insert a clove in the centre of each diamond.

In a small bowl, blend together the brown sugar, maple syrup, flour and dry mustard. Spread the brown sugar mixture over the ham. Roast for 45 minutes, brushing with the pan drippings every 15 minutes. Serve hot or cold, garnished with peach halves and parsley.

Latkes

(POTATO PANCAKES)

Makes about 20 full-sized latkes

My friend Jeff Weis of Toronto makes these crisp, flavourful latkes for
Hanukkah. At a pre-Christmas party one year, he treated some of his
non-Jewish friends to appetizer-sized mini latkes topped with sour cream
and smoked trout. Jeff recommends Yukon Gold potatoes for the latkes.

....

2½ lb (1.25 kg) potatoes (6
 medium-to-large potatoes),
 peeled
1 onion
1 egg
2 Tbsp (30 mL) all-purpose
 flour

1 tsp (5 mL) baking powder
1 tsp (5 mL) salt, preferably
 kosher
¼ tsp (1 mL) freshly ground
 black pepper

⅓ cup (75 mL) canola oil
 (approx.)
Applesauce and sour cream
 for serving

PREHEAT THE OVEN to 325°F (160°C).
Grate the potatoes and onion using the
large holes of a box grater or the coarse
shredding disc of a food processor. Enclose
in a large, clean tea towel, then gather the
ends of the towel and twist to squeeze out
as much liquid as possible.

In a medium bowl, whisk together the
egg, flour, baking powder, salt and pepper.
Add the potato mixture and mix well with
your hands. The mixture should be wet but
not soupy.

Add enough oil to a large, non-stick
skillet to cover the bottom of the skillet
by a scant ¼ inch (6 mm). Heat over
medium-high heat until a strand of the
potato mixture sizzles, but do not let the oil
smoke.

Working in batches, adding more oil as
needed and reducing the temperature if the

oil begins to smoke, drop portions of
the potato mixture into the skillet, using
¼ cup (60 mL) for full-sized latkes or
1 Tbsp (15 mL) for appetizer-sized and
patting each to flatten slightly. Fry for
2½ to 3 minutes per side, turning once,
until golden brown and cooked through.
If the raw mixture gives off any liquid
between batches, mix it to blend.

Transfer the cooked latkes to a paper-
towel-lined baking sheet to drain, then
transfer to a rack set over a baking sheet and
place in the oven to keep warm and crisp.
Serve with applesauce and sour cream. (To
make ahead, arrange the drained latkes in a
single layer on rimmed baking sheets, cover
and refrigerate for up to 8 hours. Reheat in
a 450°F/230°C oven for about 5 minutes or
until crisp and hot.)

Maple-Candied Squash

Makes 6 servings

Local squash is still available at Christmastime and makes a lovely side
that can be prepared a day or two ahead. Cool the finished dish, then
cover and refrigerate it. Bring to room temperature for 30 minutes before
reheating it in a 350°F (180°C) oven for about 20 minutes.

4 cups (1 L) mashed, cooked
  squash
¼ cup (60 mL) butter, melted
1 Tbsp (15 mL) table (18%)
  cream

½ tsp (2 mL) salt
Freshly ground black pepper
  to taste
Freshly grated nutmeg to
  taste

¼ cup (60 mL) chopped
  pecans or walnuts
2 Tbsp (30 mL) maple syrup

GREASE A 6-cup (1.5 L) casserole with
butter. Preheat the oven to 350°F (180°C).

In a medium bowl, combine the squash,
2 Tbsp (30 mL) of the melted butter, the
cream, salt, pepper and nutmeg. Spoon the
squash mixture into the prepared casserole.

In a small bowl, mix together the
remaining butter, the nuts and maple syrup.

Drizzle the butter mixture over the squash.
Bake for 20 minutes or until a glaze forms
on top.

MAPLE-CANDIED SWEET POTATOES
Follow the recipe for Maple-Candied
Squash, substituting 4 cups (1 L) mashed,
cooked sweet potatoes for the squash.

Buttery Diced Rutabaga

Makes 6 servings

Often rutabagas are waxed to help them keep longer in storage.
To remove most of the wax and make peeling easier, place the rutabaga
on some paper towels and microwave on high power for about 5 minutes.
To speed up prep time on Christmas Day, peel and dice the rutabaga
the day before, then refrigerate it in a plastic bag.

....

4 cups (1 L) peeled, diced
rutabaga

2 tsp (10 mL) firmly packed
brown sugar
¼ cup (60 mL) butter, melted

Salt and freshly ground black
pepper to taste

IN A LARGE saucepan, cover the rutabaga with boiling water and add the brown sugar. Bring to a boil, then reduce the heat and simmer, covered, for 20 to 25 minutes or until tender but not mushy.

Drain the rutabaga. Stir in the melted butter and sprinkle with salt and lots of pepper.

Acknowledgements

I would like to acknowledge the assistance of the government agencies that provided information for the original publication of this book, as well as all the special people who helped me. Family and friends from Vancouver to Halifax gleaned historical material, sent me family recipes and gave me much encouragement. A special thanks goes to Monda Rosenberg, who introduced me to the world of food writing; James Lorimer, who had faith enough in an unknown writer to publish my first book in 1979; and Elizabeth Baird, who helped me decide what to include in *The Christmas Cookbook*.

The current version, *Canadian Christmas Cooking*, came about through the enthusiastic support of Nick Rundall and the hard-working team at Whitecap. Its updated information was in the hands of my friend and meticulous editor, Julia Aitken. And finally, my thanks as always to my husband, Kent, for his help along the way.

—*Rose Murray*

About the Author

A nationally known food writer, cookbook author, broadcaster and teacher, Rose Murray has been published widely in magazines and newspapers such as *Canadian Living* and the *Globe and Mail* and has appeared on many radio and television stations across the country, including the CBC and CTV. She was the resident cook at Kitchener CTV for over twenty years. Rose is the author of eleven cookbooks; the most recent being *Canada's Favourite Recipes* (co-authored with Elizabeth Baird), which was shortlisted for the 2013 National Food Writing Award. Her tenth book, *A Taste of Canada: A Culinary Journey* (Whitecap, 2008) was shortlisted in the National Culinary Awards. Her ninth book, *Hungry for Comfort*, won gold in the 2004 National Culinary Book Awards (sponsored by Cuisine Canada and the University of Guelph). Among her other awards are the Toronto Culinary Guild's Silver Ladle Award for her unique contribution to Ontario's food industry, the Ontario Hostelry Institute's 2009 gold award as a writer and author with a focus on Canada's culinary heritage and the YWCA's 2010 Woman of Distinction for Culture award. For more information about Rose, see *Canadian Who's Who* and rosemurray.ca.

Index

S